DIABETIC
AIR FRYER
Cookbook UK

1500 Days Low-Sugar Recipes for Type 1 and 2 Diabetes - Boost Energy, Manage Blood Sugar, and Thrive! Includes Easy Meals and 4-Week Plan.

Amelia M. Parker

No part of this book may be reproduced in any form or by any electronic or mechanical means, including photocopying, recording, or by any information storage and retrieval system now known or hereafter invented, without written permission from the publisher. The only exception is by a reviewer, who may quote short excerpts in a published review.

This document is aimed to provide accurate and reliable information in the light if the selected topic and all covered issues. This book is sold with the ideas that the publisher is not required to render an officially permitted, accounting, or otherwise, qualified services. If advice is required in any way, professional or legal, seasoned experts of the profession should be consulted

Every information given herein is claimed to be consistent and truthful, in case of any liability, with regard to inattention or otherwise, by any use or abuse of processes, policies, or directions contained within is solely the responsibility of the recipient reader. Under no conditions will any blame or legal responsibility be held against the publishers for any damages, monetary loss or reparation, due to the information herein. The information herein is provided entirely for informational purposes, and it is universal.

The information is provided without any type of guarantee assurance or a contract. The trademarks that are used within the document are without any consent, and the publication of the trademark is without the backing of the trademark owner or any support. All brands and trademarks used within this book are to clarify the text only, and they are owned by their owners, not affiliated with this publication. Respective authors of this publication own all copyrights not help by the publisher.

Copyright © Amelia M. Parker

TABLE OF CONTENTS

INTRODUCTION 7
- My Journey to Discovering Diabetic Air Fryer 7
- Discussion of the Nutritional Information Provided for Each Recipe 8

PART ONE 10
- What is an Air Fryer 10
- Tips for Cooking with an Air Fryer 10
- Why Air Fryer 12
- Different Types of Air Fryer and their Costs 12
- How an Air Fryer can Benefit Diabetic Individuals 13
- Understanding Diabetes 14
- Types of Diabetes 15
- Signs of Diabetes 17
- Preventing Diabetes 17

HEADING ONEError! Bookmark not defined.

BREAKFAST 20
1. Air Fryer Apple Cinnamon Oatmeal 20
2. Air Fryer Blueberry Muffins 21
3. Air Fryer Breakfast Burritos 22
4. Air Fryer Breakfast Potatoes 23
5. Air Fryer Breakfast Quiche 24
6. Air Fryer Breakfast Tacos 25
7. Air Fryer Breakfast Stuffed Peppers 26
8. Air Fryer Egg and Sausage Breakfast Sandwich 27
9. Air Fryer French Toast 28
10. Air Fryer Ham and Cheese Croissants 29
11. Air Fryer Breakfast Sandwich 30
12. Air Fryer Breakfast Sausage 31
13. Air Fryer Breakfast Scramble 32
14. Air Fryer Breakfast Smoothie 33
15. Air Fryer Breakfast Wrap 34
16. Air Fryer Breakfast Quinoa 35
17. Air Fryer Breakfast Yogurt 36
18. Air Fryer Breakfast Omelette 37
19. Air Fryer Breakfast Frittata 38
20. Air Fryer Breakfast Crepes 39
21. Air Fryer Breakfast Waffles 40
22. Air Fryer Breakfast Pancakes 41
23. Air Fryer Breakfast Strata 42
24. Air Fryer Breakfast Biscuit 43
25. Air Fryer Breakfast Hash 44
26. Air Fryer Breakfast Croquette 45
27. Air Fryer Breakfast Churro 46
28. Air Fryer Breakfast Muffin 47
29. Air Fryer Breakfast Scones 48
30. Air Fryer Breakfast Parfait 49

HEADING ONEError! Bookmark not defined.

LUNCH 51
1. Air Fryer Baked Potatoes 51
2. Air Fryer Chicken Fajitas 52
3. Air Fryer Eggplant Parmesan 53
4. Air Fryer Grilled Cheese Sandwich 54
5. Air Fryer Grilled Vegetable Skewers 55
6. Air Fryer Roasted Asparagus 56
7. Air Fryer Salmon Cakes 57
8. Air Fryer Shrimp Tacos 58
9. Air Fryer Spinach and Cheese Frittata 59
10. Air Fryer Steak Fries 60
11. Avocado and Egg Salad 61
12. Baked Apple Chips 62
13. Baked Sweet Potato Fries 63
14. Broccoli and Cheese Stuffed Portobellos 64
15. Chicken and Quinoa Bowls 65
16. Chicken and Veggie Stir Fry 66
17. Chili-Lime Tofu 67

18. Crispy Baked Tofu 68
19. Curried Vegetable Soup 69
20. Egg and Cheese Rollups 70
21. Falafel Wraps 71
22. Greek Salad with Grilled Chicken 72
23. Grilled Cheese and Tomato Sandwich .. 73
24. Kale and White Bean Soup 74
25. Lentil and Vegetable Stew 75
26. Loaded Sweet Potato Skins 76
27. Roasted Chickpeas 77
28. Roasted Veggie and Quinoa Salad 78
29. Skinny French Toast Sticks 79
30. Vegetable and Bean Burritos 80

PART FOUR 81

Dinner 81

1. Air Fryer Sesame Chicken 81
2. Air Fryer Cauliflower Wings 82
3. Air Fryer Lemon Garlic Shrimp 83
4. Air Fryer Meatball Subs 84
5. Air Fryer Parmesan Crusted Pork Chops 85
6. Air Fryer Stuffed Bell Peppers 86
7. Air Fryer Teriyaki Tofu 87
8. Air Fryer Zucchini Fries 88
9. Black Bean and Sweet Potato Tacos 89
10. Air Fryer BBQ Pork Tenderloin 90
11. Air Fryer Crispy Tofu Nuggets 91
12. Air Fryer Harissa Chicken Skewers 92

13. Air Fryer Mushroom and Onion Quiche 93
14. Air Fryer Pesto Chicken 94
15. Air Fryer Rosemary Roasted Potatoes .. 95
16. Air Fryer Spicy Tuna Rolls 96
17. Air Fryer Spinach and Feta Stuffed Chicken Breasts 97
18. Air Fryer Turkey Meatballs 98
19. Air Fryer Vegetable and Tofu Korma 99
20. Edamame and Avocado Salad 100
21. Skinny Cauliflower Mac and Cheese ... 101
22. Vegetable and Quinoa Shepherd's Pie 102
23. Orange and Almond Tofu Stir-fry 103
24. Air Fryer Cajun-spiced Catfish 104
25. Lightened-up Broccoli and Cheese Soup 105
26. Turkey and Vegetable Meatloaf 106
27. Air Fryer Turkey and Vegetable Chili ... 107
28. Grilled Lemon-Garlic Chicken and Vegetables 108
29. Air Fryer Sausage and Pepper Hoagies 109
30. Chicken and Vegetable Paella 110

CONCLUSION 111

The Benefits of Using an Air Fryer for Diabetic Cooking 111

Key Takeaways from the Book 112

Tips and Tricks for Using an Air Fryer Effectively in Diabetic Cooking 113

Personal Reflection 114

INTRODUCTION

My Journey to Discovering Diabetic Air Fryer

My journey to discovering the diabetic air fryer started when I was diagnosed with diabetes. I was devastated at first, feeling like I had to give up all of my favorite foods and that my life would be over. My doctor reassured me that I could still enjoy food, but I had to be careful with my blood sugar levels. I was worried that I would never be able to enjoy the same foods I used to eat, so I started researching different methods of cooking that were diabetes-friendly.

That's when I discovered the diabetic air fryer. The air fryer uses hot air to quickly and evenly cook food without all the added fat and calories. I was amazed at all the different recipes I could make with the air fryer, and I decided to give it a try. After a few weeks of experimenting, I was hooked! I was able to make all kinds of delicious meals that were diabetes-friendly, and I no longer had to worry about my health while I enjoyed them.

The diabetic air fryer has been a life saver for me. I can now enjoy all my favorite foods without worrying about my health. I also love how quick and easy it is to use. Meal prep is a breeze now, and I'm able to whip up delicious meals in no time. I'm so glad I made the switch to the diabetic air fryer, and I'm sure it has changed my life for the better. But the benefits of the diabetic air fryer go beyond just helping me to manage my diabetes. It has also made it much easier for me to prepare healthy meals at home. I can cook chicken, fish, and vegetables to perfection without the need for added oil or butter. And because it cooks food quickly and evenly, I can have dinner on the table in no time.

If you are living with diabetes, I highly recommend considering the diabetic air fryer as a tool in your journey to manage your condition. It has made a huge difference in my life and I am confident it can do the same for you. Not only it can help you manage diabetes it also makes it easy to cook healthy and delicious meals at home.

Discussion of the Nutritional Information Provided for Each Recipe

The "Diabetic Air Fryer Cookbook for Beginners" provides readers with detailed nutritional information for each recipe, making it an essential guide for individuals with diabetes who are looking to improve their dietary habits and manage their blood sugar levels. The nutritional information includes information on calories, carbohydrates, protein, fat, and other important nutrients. This allows readers to make informed decisions about what they eat and ensure that their meals align with their dietary goals.

The book provides guidance on how to use nutritional information to adapt recipes to fit individual dietary needs. For example, for those who are following a low-carb or ketogenic diet, the book provides suggestions for substituting ingredients to reduce the carbohydrate content of recipes.

The inclusion of nutritional information in the recipes makes it easy for readers to plan their meals and make sure they are getting the right balance of nutrients. It also allows readers to track their progress, and make adjustments as needed.

The "Diabetic Air Fryer Cookbook for Beginners" provides readers with detailed nutritional information for each recipe, allowing them to make informed decisions about what they eat and ensure that their meals align with their dietary goals. This makes the book an essential guide for individuals with diabetes who are looking to improve their dietary habits and manage their blood sugar levels.

Brace Yourself

The book is filled with high-quality images that make it easy to understand and follow the recipes. Each recipe is accompanied by a beautiful image of the finished dish, making it easy to see what you are working towards as you cook.

In addition to the images, the book also includes detailed nutritional information for each recipe. This is extremely helpful for those managing diabetes, as it allows them to easily keep track of their carbohydrate, protein, and fat intake. The nutritional information is presented in an easy-to-read format, making it simple to understand and use.

One of the most impressive features of the book is its organization. The recipes are arranged in alphabetical order, making it easy to find the dish you are looking for. This organization makes it simple to quickly flip through the book and find the recipe you want, saving you time and hassle in the kitchen.

Overall, this book is a must-have for anyone living with diabetes. Its combination of quality images, detailed nutritional information, and alphabetical organization makes it a valuable resource for managing diabetes and cooking delicious, healthy meals. It's a great tool for anyone looking to control diabetes, improve their diet and cook delicious and healthy meals.

PART ONE

What is an Air Fryer

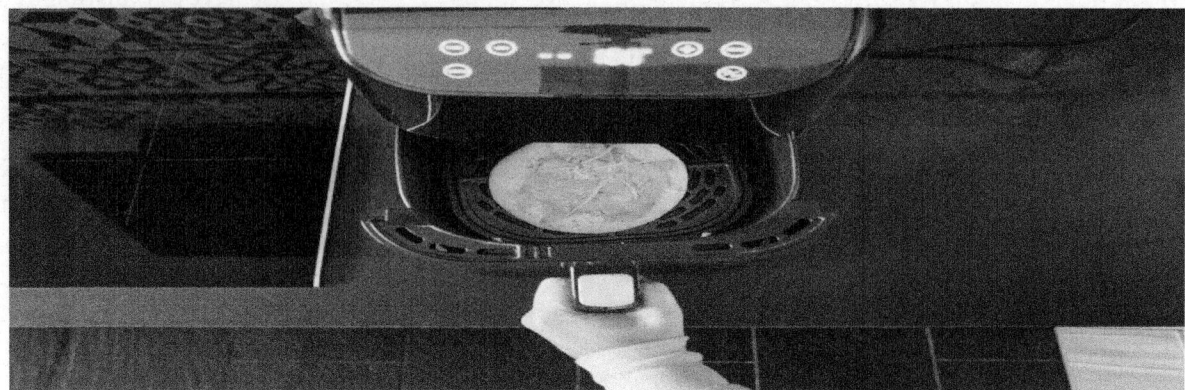

An air fryer is a kitchen appliance that utilizes a convection-like circulation of hot air to fry, bake or roast food. It works by circulating hot air around the food, creating a crispy exterior and evenly cooking the food. A heating element generates the hot air, and the food is placed in a basket or tray suspended in the air fryer.

The food is cooked by the hot air that is circulated around it, which creates a crispy exterior and cooks the food evenly. Unlike deep-frying, which uses oil to cook food, an air fryer uses little to no oil, making it a healthier alternative. Some popular foods that can be cooked in an air fryer include French fries, chicken, fish, and vegetables. It can also be used for baking, roasting, and grilling.

Tips for Cooking with an Air Fryer

Whether you're a seasoned pro or new to the world of air frying. **There are some tips to help you get the most out of your air fryer:**

- Preheat your air fryer before cooking. This will ensure that your food cooks evenly and quickly.

- Use a light coating of oil or cooking spray to help your food crisp up. Keep in mind that you only need a small amount of oil, as the hot air circulating in the air fryer will do most of the work.

- Be mindful of the size of your food. Cut food into even-sized pieces to ensure that they cook evenly.
- Shake your food halfway through cooking. This will help distribute the hot air and ensure that your food cooks evenly.
- Use the right accessories. Some air fryers come with special trays and racks that can be used to cook different types of food. For example, a tray with raised edges is perfect for cooking French fries, while a rack is ideal for cooking chicken wings.
- Experiment with different cooking times and temperatures. Different foods will require different cooking times and temperatures. For example, chicken wings may need to cook for 20 minutes at 400 degrees, while French fries may only need to cook for 15 minutes at 375 degrees.
- Don't overcrowd the air fryer. Make sure that there is enough space for the hot air to circulate around your food, otherwise, it will take longer to cook.
- Make sure your food is dry before placing it in the air fryer. Any excess moisture will prevent your food from crisping up.
- Try marinating your food before air frying. This will add flavor and help keep the food moist.
- Have fun and experiment. Air frying is a versatile cooking method that allows you to cook a wide range of foods. Don't be afraid to try new recipes and ingredients.
- Cooking with an air fryer is a fun and easy way to make delicious and healthy meals. With a little practice and these tips, you'll be a pro in no time.

Why Air Fryer

In recent years, Air fryers have gained immense popularity due to their multitude of benefits. They offer a healthier alternative to traditional deep-frying methods by using little to no oil, while still producing crispy and delicious food. But the benefits of an air fryer go beyond just being a healthier option.

One of the main advantages of using an air fryer is its ability to cook food quickly and evenly. The hot air circulating inside the fryer cooks food from all sides, resulting in crispy and golden brown food in a fraction of the time it would take to cook in a traditional oven. This not only saves time but also energy as the air fryer uses less power than a traditional oven.

Air fryers are also a great option for people looking to eat healthier. Traditional deep-frying methods can add a lot of excess oil and calories to food, whereas air fryers allow you to cook with very little oil, significantly reducing the fat content of your food. In addition, air fryers are also great for people with dietary restrictions, such as gluten-free or vegan diets. They can be used to make a variety of gluten-free and vegan-friendly dishes.

Another benefit of air fryers is their versatility. They can be used to cook a wide range of foods, from French fries and chicken wings to vegetables and even desserts. The temperature and time can be adjusted to suit the specific food, making it easy to achieve the perfect level of crispiness. Many air fryers also come with accessories such as trays and racks that can be used to cook different types of food, adding to the versatility of the appliance. Air fryers are also easy to use and clean. They have simple controls and most models have dishwasher-safe parts, making cleanup a breeze. Plus, since they use very little oil, there is less mess and splatters to deal with.

Air fryers are a convenient, versatile, and healthy cooking option that offers a wide range of benefits. They are easy to use, easy to clean and allow you to enjoy delicious and crispy food with little to no oil. With the many advantages air fryers offer, it's no wonder they are becoming a staple in many kitche

Different Types of Air Fryer and their Costs

There are several types of air fryers available on the market, each with its own unique features and capabilities. **Here are a few of the most common types and their approximate costs:**

Countertop air fryers: These are the most common type of air fryer and range in size from 2-6 quarts. They sit on your countertop and have a basket or tray where the food is placed. Prices for these types of air fryers range from $30 to $200, depending on the brand and features.

Toaster oven air fryers: These air fryers are designed to look like traditional toaster ovens but with the added feature of air frying capabilities. They typically have a larger capacity than countertop air fryers and can hold multiple trays or racks. They tend to be more expensive, with prices ranging from $100 to $300.

Multi-cooker air fryers: These air fryers also have other cooking functions such as pressure cooking, steaming, sautéing, and more. They tend to be larger and more expensive than countertop air fryers, with prices ranging from $150 to $400.

Built-in air fryers: These are built into the wall of your kitchen, like a microwave, and are typically installed by a professional. These air fryers are the most expensive, with prices ranging from $1000 to $3000.

Portable air fryers: These air fryers are designed to be taken on the go and are smaller than traditional countertop air fryers. They are also less expensive, with prices ranging from $30 to $100

Keep in mind that the cost of an air fryer is not the only factor to consider when making a purchase. You should also take into account the size and features that are important to you, as well as the brands available in your area. Additionally, it's also important to read reviews from other customers before making a final decision.

How an Air Fryer can Benefit Diabetic Individuals

One of the key aspects of managing diabetes is maintaining a healthy diet, which can be challenging for many people, especially when it comes to the foods they love. Fried foods, in particular, are often high in calories, fat, and carbohydrates and can be a problem for diabetic individuals. However, this is where the air fryer comes in as a game changer.

One of the main benefits of an air fryer for diabetic individuals is that it allows them to enjoy their favorite fried foods without the added fat and calories. For example, instead of deep-frying French fries in oil, which can add hundreds of calories and grams of fat, they can be cooked in an air fryer with just a mist of oil and still have that crispy texture and taste. This can be a great way to enjoy a treat without compromising blood sugar levels.

In addition to allowing diabetic individuals to enjoy fried foods, an air fryer can also be used to prepare a wide variety of healthy meals. It can be used to cook lean proteins such as chicken, fish, and turkey breast, as well as a variety of vegetables. These foods are not only low in fat and calories but also high in nutrients, which can help to support overall health.

Moreover, an air fryer can also be used to prepare meals quickly and easily, which can be helpful for people who have busy schedules. It can cook a variety of meals in a fraction of the time it would take to prepare them in a traditional oven, and it also reduces the need for constant monitoring and stirring, which makes it a convenient kitchen tool.

An air fryer can also be used to prepare meals in a healthier way than other cooking methods. For example, instead of grilling or pan-frying chicken, which can add extra fat, an air fryer can cook chicken breast with little to no added oil. This can help to reduce the overall fat and calorie content of the meal.

An air fryer also makes clean-up easy and fast, as the food is cooked in a basket and requires little to no oil. This reduces the amount of mess and makes it simple to clean. Air fryer is a valuable tool for diabetic individuals looking to maintain a healthy diet. It allows them to enjoy their favorite fried foods without the added fat and calories, and it can also be used to prepare a wide variety of healthy meals quickly and easily. It also allows for more beneficial cooking methods and easy clean-up. If you're living with diabetes, it's worth considering adding an air fryer to your kitchen. It can make a big difference in your life and help you manage your condition more effectively.

Understanding Diabetes

Millions of people around the world suffer from diabetes, a long-term health condition. It occurs when the body is unable to properly use and store glucose (a type of sugar) as energy. Type 2 diabetes, also known as adult-onset diabetes, is a metabolic disorder that is characterized by high levels of sugar in the blood. It is caused by the body's inability to produce enough insulin or to effectively use the insulin it does produce. As a result, individuals with type 1 diabetes must take insulin injections or use an insulin pump to regulate their blood sugar levels. Type 1 diabetes can be seen at any age, although it is typically diagnosed in childhood or adolescence.

In contrast, Type 2 Diabetes is the most commonly diagnosed form of diabetes. It is caused by the body's resistance to insulin or lack of insulin production. This results in high blood sugar levels, which can lead to serious health complications if not properly managed. Type 2 diabetes is often linked to obesity and lack of physical activity, and it is more common in older adults, but it can also occur in younger people. In both types of diabetes, high blood sugar levels can cause a variety of health problems, including heart disease, nerve damage, kidney damage, and blindness. Additionally, diabetes can also increase the risk of developing certain cancers.

Managing diabetes requires a combination of lifestyle changes and medical treatments. The key aspect of managing diabetes is maintaining a healthy diet. Consuming a diversity of nutrient-rich foods, such as fruits, vegetables, whole grains, lean proteins, and healthy fats while limiting processed and high-fat foods, sugary drinks, and added sugars. Additionally, regular physical activity is also crucial for managing diabetes, as it can help to lower blood sugar levels and improve overall health.

Medications, such as insulin and oral diabetes medications, may also be necessary to help regulate blood sugar levels. Additionally, regular monitoring of blood sugar levels is important to ensure they remain within a healthy range.

Managing diabetes can be a challenging task, but with the right tools and support, it is possible to live a healthy and fulfilling life. It is important to work closely with a healthcare team, including a doctor, a diabetes educator, and a dietitian, to develop a personalized plan for managing diabetes. Additionally, support from family and friends, as well as diabetes support groups, can be a valuable resource for individuals with diabetes.

It is important to work closely with a healthcare team, maintain a healthy diet, engage in regular physical activity, and take medications as prescribed, to manage diabetes effectively.

Types of Diabetes

- Type 1 diabetes
- Type 2 diabetes
- Gestational diabetes
- Latent autoimmune diabetes in adults (LADA)
- Maturity onset diabetes of the young (MODY)
- Monogenic diabetes
- Secondary diabetes
- Neonatal diabetes
- Drug-induced diabetes
- Genetic defects of beta cell function
- Genetic defects in insulin action

Please note that this list is not exhaustive and new types of diabetes are being discovered and studied. Also, some of the above types may be considered subtypes of the main three types and may not be recognized as a separate types by all medical communities.

Type 1 Diabetes

Often referred to as juvenile diabetes, Type 1 Diabetes is an autoimmune disorder in which the body's immune system mistakenly identifies and attacks the cells that produce insulin, leading to their destruction. Insulin is a hormone that is responsible for regulating blood sugar levels. As a result, individuals with type 1 diabetes must take insulin injections or use an insulin pump to regulate their blood sugar levels. Type 1 diabetes usually develops in childhood or adolescence, but it can occur at any age.

Type 2 Diabetes

This is the most common type of diabetes and occurs when the body becomes resistant to insulin or doesn't produce enough insulin. This results in high blood sugar levels, which can lead to serious health complications if not properly managed. Type 2 diabetes is often linked to obesity and lack of physical activity, and it is more common in older adults, but it can also occur in younger people.

Gestational Diabetes

Also known as pregnancy diabetes, it is a type of diabetes that develops during pregnancy. It occurs when the body cannot produce enough insulin to meet the increased demand during pregnancy. It usually goes away after giving birth, but it increases the risk of developing type 2 diabetes later in life, and the baby can also be at risk of health issues.

Latent Autoimmune Diabetes in Adults (LADA)

It is also known as type 1.5 diabetes, it is a form of diabetes that is characterized by the presence of autoantibodies against the insulin-producing beta cells in the pancreas. It is considered a slow-progressing form of type 1 diabetes, symptoms usually appear in adulthood, and is often misdiagnosed as type 2 diabetes.

Maturity Onset Diabetes of the Young (MODY)

It is a rare form of diabetes characterized by early onset and strong family history. It is caused by a genetic defect that affects the insulin-producing cells in the pancreas. It is different from type 1 and type 2 diabetes, as it does not require insulin therapy and tends to have a less severe course.

Monogenic Diabetes

Is a rare form of diabetes that is caused by alterations in a single gene? It is characterized by early onset and often does not require insulin therapy. The most common types of monogenic diabetes are maturity-onset diabetes of the young (MODY) and neonatal diabetes.

Secondary Diabetes

It is a type of diabetes that results from another medical condition or from certain medications, such as steroids. It can occur when the pancreas is damaged or when the body's hormone system is disrupted. This type of diabetes is often temporary and can be treated by addressing the underlying condition or discontinuing the medication.

Neonatal Diabetes

It is a rare form of diabetes that occurs in infants and young children. It is caused by genetic defects in the insulin-producing cells in the pancreas, and it usually requires insulin therapy.

Drug-induced Diabetes

It is a type of diabetes that can occur as a side effect of certain medications, such as steroids, antipsychotics, and beta-blockers. Diabetes usually resolves when the medication is discontinued.

Genetic Defects of Beta Cell Function

This type of diabetes is caused by genetic defects that affect the function of the insulin-producing beta cells in the pancreas. It can be inherited and can manifest in different forms, such as maturity-onset diabetes of the young (MODY) or neonatal diabetes.

Genetic Defects in Insulin Action

This type of diabetes is caused by genetic defects that affect the way the body uses insulin. It can manifest in different forms, such as inherited forms of type 2 diabetes. It's important to note that diabetes can have many different causes and forms. And a proper diagnosis is crucial for proper treatment and management. It's also important to work closely with a healthcare team, including a doctor, a diabetes educator, and a dietitian, to develop a personalized plan for managing diabetes.

Type 1 diabetes is a condition in which the body's immune system mistakenly attacks and destroys the cells in the pancreas that produce insulin, resulting in the body not being able to produce insulin. Type 2 diabetes occurs when the body does not use insulin properly, resulting in high levels of blood sugar. Both types of diabetes can lead to serious health complications, including heart disease, stroke, blindness, and kidney disease. Treatment for diabetes includes lifestyle changes such as healthy eating, physical activity, and medication. While both types share similar symptoms, they have different causes and risk factors.

Signs of Diabetes

One of the most common signs of diabetes is frequent urination. When blood sugar levels are high, the kidneys work overtime to filter out the excess sugar, which can cause an increase in urine production. As a result, people with diabetes may find themselves needing to use the bathroom more frequently, especially at night.

Another common sign of diabetes is increased thirst and dry mouth. High blood sugar levels can cause the body to lose fluids, leading to dehydration and increased thirst. This can also cause dryness in the mouth, eyes, and skin.

Diabetes can lead to feelings of fatigue and weakness. High blood sugar levels can cause the body to produce more insulin, which can lead to a decrease in energy levels. People with diabetes may also experience tingling or numbness in their hands and feet, which is caused by nerve damage caused by high blood sugar levels.

Weight loss can also be a sign of diabetes, especially in type 1 diabetes. The body may start breaking down fat and muscle for energy when the body doesn't have enough insulin to use glucose (sugar) from the bloodstream.

Blurred vision is another symptom of diabetes, caused by changes in the shape of the lens in the eye due to high blood sugar levels.

Slow-healing wounds and infections are also common in people with diabetes. High blood sugar levels can damage the blood vessels and nerves, which can affect the body's ability to fight off infections and heal wounds.

If you are experiencing any of these symptoms, it's important to see a healthcare professional to get your blood sugar levels checked. Early diagnosis and treatment can help prevent serious complications associated with diabetes.

It's also important to note that many people with type 2 diabetes may not have any symptoms at all, or they may develop symptoms gradually over time. It's important to get regular check-ups, especially if you are at risk of developing diabetes. Risk factors include being overweight, having a family history of diabetes, being over the age of 45, and having high blood pressure.

Preventing Diabetes

One of the most effective ways to prevent diabetes is to maintain a healthy weight. Being overweight or obese is one of the leading risk factors for diabetes, as excess weight can lead to insulin resistance and an increased risk of high blood sugar levels. To maintain a healthy weight, it is important to eat a balanced diet that is high in fruits, vegetables, and whole grains, and low in processed foods and added sugars. It is also important to engage in regular physical activity, as regular exercise can help to burn calories and boost insulin sensitivity.

Another important step in the prevention of diabetes is to manage stress levels. Stress can lead to an increase in blood sugar levels, as well as an increase in the risk of developing diabetes. To manage stress levels, individuals can try practices such as yoga, meditation, and deep breathing. Additionally, it is important to get enough sleep each night, as lack of sleep can increase the risk of diabetes and other health problems.

It is also important to manage other risk factors for diabetes, such as high blood pressure and high cholesterol. These conditions can be managed through a healthy diet, regular physical activity, and medication as prescribed by a healthcare professional. Regular check-ups with a healthcare provider can also help to identify any risk factors early on and take steps to prevent diabetes.

In addition to these lifestyle changes, individuals can also take steps to prevent diabetes by making sure they are getting enough vitamins and minerals. Vitamin D and magnesium, for example, have been shown to play a role in the prevention of diabetes. These can be obtained through food, supplements, or sunlight.

It is important to remember that preventing diabetes is a lifelong process, and it is important to stay committed to making healthy lifestyle changes. By eating well, staying active, managing stress, and taking steps to prevent other risk factors, individuals can significantly reduce their risk of developing diabetes and improve their overall health and well-being.

Diabetes is a serious health condition that can have serious complications. However, by making certain lifestyle changes and managing the risk factors, individuals can reduce their risk of developing diabetes and enjoy a healthier, happier life. With a little effort and some determination, we can all take steps to prevent diabetes and live our best lives.

BREAKFAST
1. Air Fryer Apple Cinnamon Oatmeal

Ingredients

- 1 cup rolled oats

- 1 cup unsweetened almond milk

- 1/2 cup diced apples

- 1 tablespoon honey or maple syrup

- 1 teaspoon cinnamon

- /4 teaspoon nutmeg

- Pinch of salt

Optional toppings: chopped nuts, dried fruit, and extra cinnamon

Instructions

1. In a medium bowl, combine the rolled oats, almond milk, diced apples, honey or maple syrup, cinnamon, nutmeg, and salt. Stir well to combine.
2. Place the oatmeal mixture in the air fryer basket and set the temperature to 350 degrees Fahrenheit. Cook for 10-15 minutes, or until the oatmeal is cooked through and lightly golden brown on top.
3. Remove the oatmeal from the air fryer and top it with your desired toppings. Serve hot and enjoy.

Note: You can adjust the cooking time depending on your air fryer, you can also add more or less of the sweeteners, or add more or less spices to your preference.

Nutritional Information

Below is an estimate of the nutritional information per serving of the basic recipe (without any additional toppings):

- Calories: 150 - Fat: 2.5g - Saturated Fat: 0.5g - Cholesterol: 0mg - Sodium: 50mg - Carbohydrates: 27g - Fiber: 3g- Sugar: 10g - Protein: 4g

2. Air Fryer Blueberry Muffins

Ingredients

- 1 1/2 cups all-purpose flour
- 3/4 cup granulated sugar
- 2 teaspoons baking powder
- 1/2 teaspoon salt
- 1/2 cup unsalted butter, melted
- 2 large eggs
- 1/2 cup milk
- 1 teaspoon vanilla extract
- 1 cup fresh blueberries

Instructions

- In a large bowl, mix together the flour, sugar, baking powder, and salt. Then, in a separate bowl, whisk together the melted butter, eggs, milk, and vanilla extract.
- Slowly add the wet ingredients to the dry ingredients and stir until just combined. Fold in the blueberries.
- Grease the muffin cups of the air fryer basket. Using a large spoon or cookie scoop, fill the muffin cups with the batter, leaving a little room at the top for the muffins to rise.
- Place the muffin cups in the air fryer and set the temperature to 350 degrees Fahrenheit. Cook for 15-20 minutes, or until a toothpick inserted into the center of a muffin comes out clean.
- Remove the muffins from the air fryer and let them cool for a few minutes before serving.

Note: You can adjust the cooking time depending on your air fryer.

Nutritional information (per serving, based on 12 muffins):

- Calories: 200
- Fat: 11g
- Saturated Fat: 6g
- Cholesterol: 55mg
- Sodium: 150mg
- Carbohydrates: 25g
- Fiber: 1g
- Sugar: 14g
- Protein: 3g

3. Air Fryer Breakfast Burritos

Ingredients

- 1 1/2 cups all-purpose flour
- 3/4 cup granulated sugar
- 2 teaspoons baking powder
- 1/2 teaspoon salt
- 1/2 cup unsalted butter, melted
- 2 large eggs
- 1/2 cup milk
- 1 teaspoon vanilla extract
- 1 cup fresh blueberries

Instructions

1. In a large bowl, mix together the flour, sugar, baking powder, and salt. Then, in a separate bowl, whisk together the melted butter, eggs, milk, and vanilla extract.
2. Slowly add the wet ingredients to the dry ingredients and stir until just combined. Fold in the blueberries.
3. Grease the muffin cups of the air fryer basket. Using a large spoon or cookie scoop, fill the muffin cups with the batter, leaving a little room at the top for the muffins to rise.
4. Place the muffin cups in the air fryer and set the temperature to 350 degrees Fahrenheit. Cook for 15-20 minutes, or until a toothpick inserted into the center of a muffin comes out clean.
5. Remove the muffins from the air fryer and let them cool for a few minutes before serving.

Note: You can adjust the cooking time depending on your air fryer.

Nutritional information (per serving, based on 12 muffins):

- Calories: 200 - Fat: 11g - Saturated Fat: 6g - Cholesterol: 55mg - Sodium: 150mg - Carbohydrates: 25g - Fiber: 1g - Sugar: 14g - Protein: 3g

4. Air Fryer Breakfast Potatoes

Ingredients

- 2 medium russet potatoes, diced
- 1 tablespoon olive oil
- 1 teaspoon paprika
- 1/2 teaspoon garlic powder
- 1/4 teaspoon salt
- 1/4 teaspoon black pepper
- Optional: chopped fresh herbs such as parsley or chives, for garnish

Instructions

1. Combine the diced potatoes, olive oil, paprika, garlic powder, salt, and pepper in a large bowl and mix until all ingredients are evenly distributed.
2. Place the potatoes in the air fryer basket and cook at 375 degrees Fahrenheit for 20-25 minutes, or until golden brown and crispy. Stir the contents of the basket every 5 to 7 minutes to guarantee an even cooking process.
3. Remove the potatoes from the air fryer and sprinkle them with chopped fresh herbs, if desired. Serve immediately.

Note: You can adjust the cooking time depending on your air fryer.

Nutritional information (per serving, based on 4 servings): - Calories: 140 - Fat: 6g - Saturated Fat: 1g - Cholesterol: 0mg - Sodium: 210mg - Carbohydrates: 20g - Fiber: 2g - Sugar: 1g - Protein: 2g

5. Air Fryer Breakfast Quiche

Ingredients

- 1 9-inch refrigerated pie crust
- 1 cup diced cooked ham
- 1 cup shredded cheddar cheese
- 1/2 cup diced onion
- 1/2 cup diced bell pepper
- 6 eggs
- 1/2 cup milk
- Salt and pepper to taste

Instructions

1 Set the air fryer to a temperature of 350 degrees Fahrenheit.

2 Place the pie crust in the air fryer basket.

3 In a bowl, mix together the diced ham, cheese that has been shredded, a diced onion, and a diced bell pepper.

4 Distribute the mixture uniformly throughout the pie crust.

5 In a different bowl, combine the eggs and milk. Add salt and pepper to taste.

6 Pour the egg mixture over the ham and cheese mixture into the pie crust.

7 Carefully place the pie crust in the air fryer basket.

8 Cook for 15-20 minutes or until the quiche is set and the crust is golden brown.

9 Let cool for a few minutes before slicing and serving.

Nutritional information per serving (based on 8 servings per quiche):

- Calories: 254
- Fat: 18g
- Carbohydrates: 12g
- Protein: 12g
- Sodium: 400mg
- Cholesterol: 141mg

6. Air Fryer Breakfast Tacos

Ingredients

- 1 cup diced cooked breakfast sausage
- 1 cup diced potatoes
- 1/2 cup diced onion
- 8 corn tortillas
- 1/2 cup diced bell pepper
- 1 cup shredded cheddar cheese
- Salt and pepper to taste

Instructions

1 Set the air fryer to 400°F.

2 In a mixing bowl, combine the diced breakfast sausage, diced potatoes, diced onion, and diced bell pepper. Season with salt and pepper.

3 Put the 4 tortillas in the air fryer basket.

4 Spoon the sausage and potato mixture over the tortillas, spreading it out evenly.

5 Cover each tortilla with shredded cheese.

6 Place the remaining 4 tortillas on top of the cheese, pressing down gently to create a sandwich.

7 Carefully place the tacos in the air fryer basket.

8 Cook for 5-7 minutes or until the tortillas are crispy and the cheese is melted.

9 Carefully remove the tacos from the air fryer and let them cool for a few minutes before slicing and serving.

Nutritional information per serving (based on 4 servings per recipe):

- Calories: 383
- Fat: 22g
- Carbohydrates: 26g
- Protein: 16g
- Sodium: 742mg
- Cholesterol: 45mg

7. Air Fryer Breakfast Stuffed Peppers

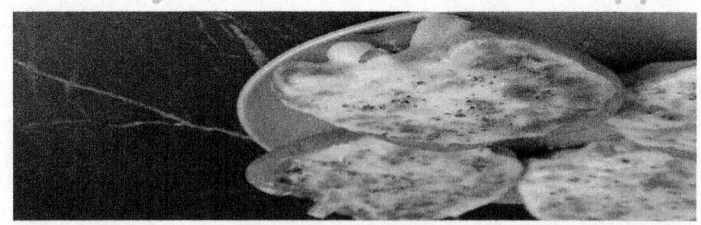

Ingredients

-4 bell peppers (red, yellow, or green)

-1 cup cooked quinoa

-1 cup diced cooked breakfast sausage

-1/2 cup diced onion

-1/2 cup diced tomato

-1/2 cup shredded cheddar cheese

-Salt and pepper to taste

Instructions

1. Set the air fryer to a temperature of 400 degrees Fahrenheit.
2. Slice the tops off the bell peppers, discarding the stems. Discard the seeds and membranes inside the peppers.
3. In a mixing bowl, combine the cooked quinoa, diced breakfast sausage, diced onion, and diced tomato. Season with salt and pepper.
4. Stuff each bell pepper with the quinoa and sausage mixture.
5. Put the bell peppers into the air fryer basket.
6. Cook for 15-20 minutes or until the peppers are tender and the filling is hot.
7. Sprinkle shredded cheese over each pepper.
8. Cook for an additional 2-3 minutes or until the cheese is melted.
9. Carefully remove the peppers from the air fryer and let them cool for a few minutes before serving.

Nutritional information per serving (based on 4 servings per recipe): - Calories: 298 - Fat: 16g - Carbohydrates: 23g - Protein: 14g - Sodium: 447mg - Cholesterol: 45mg

8. Air Fryer Egg and Sausage Breakfast Sandwich

Ingredients

-2 English muffins, split and toasted

-4 eggs

-4 breakfast sausages

-1/4 cup shredded cheddar cheese

-Salt and pepper to taste

Instructions

1 Set the air fryer to 400°F.

2 Place the breakfast sausages in the air fryer basket.

3 Cook the eggs for 3 to 5 minutes, or until they are cooked through but still moist.

4 Remove the sausages from the air fryer basket and set them aside.

5 Crack the eggs into the air fryer basket, and season with salt and pepper.

6 Heat a pan over medium heat and add the eggs. Cook the eggs for 3-5 minutes, stirring occasionally, until they are set but still moist.

7 Remove the eggs from the air fryer basket and set them aside.

8 On the bottom half of each toasted English muffin, place a cooked sausage patty and a cooked egg.

9 Sprinkle shredded cheese over the top of the eggs.

10 Place the sandwiches back into the air fryer basket and cook for an additional 2-3 minutes or until the cheese is melted.

11 Carefully remove the sandwiches from the air fryer and let them cool for a few minutes before serving.

Nutritional information per serving (based on 2 servings per recipe):

- Calories: 538

- Fat: 34g

- Carbohydrates: 34g

- Protein: 23g

- Sodium: 1149mg

- Cholesterol: 347mg

9. Air Fryer French Toast

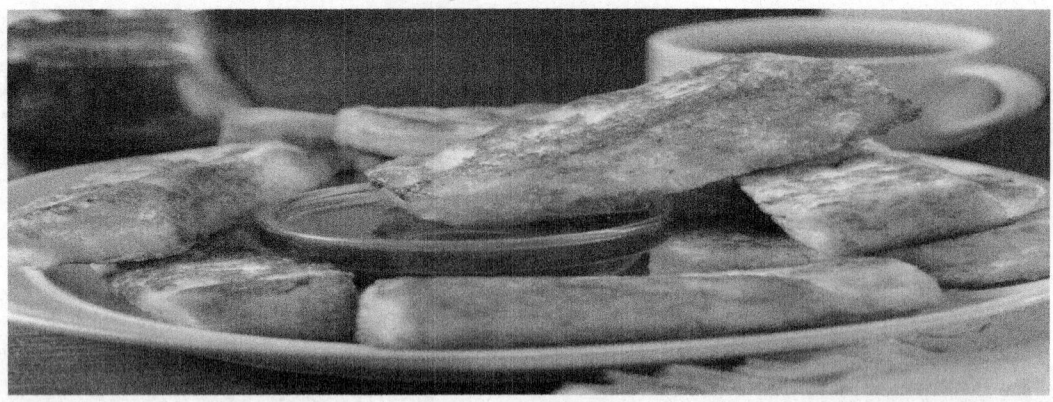

Ingredients

- 4 slices of thick bread (such as Texas toast or challah)
- 2 eggs
- 1/2 cup milk
- 1 tsp vanilla extract
- 1/4 tsp cinnamon
- 1/4 tsp nutmeg
- Pinch of salt
- Butter or oil spray, for coating the air fryer basket
- Maple syrup and powdered sugar for serving (optional)

Instructions

1. Set the air fryer to 400°F.
2. In a shallow dish, combine the eggs, milk, vanilla extract, cinnamon, nutmeg, and salt. Whisk them together until blended.
3. Dip the bread slices into the egg mixture, allowing them to soak for a minute or two on each side.
4. Lightly coat the air fryer basket with butter or oil spray.
5. Put the slices of bread into the air fryer's basket.
6. Cook for 8-10 minutes or until the bread is golden brown and the edges are crispy.
7. Carefully remove the French toast from the air fryer and let cool for a few minutes before serving.
8. If desired, serve with maple syrup and powdered sugar.

Nutritional information per serving (based on 4 servings per recipe):

Calories: 174

Fat: 7g

Carbohydrates: 21g

Protein: 6g

Sodium: 267mg

Cholesterol: 120mg

10. Air Fryer Ham and Cheese Croissants

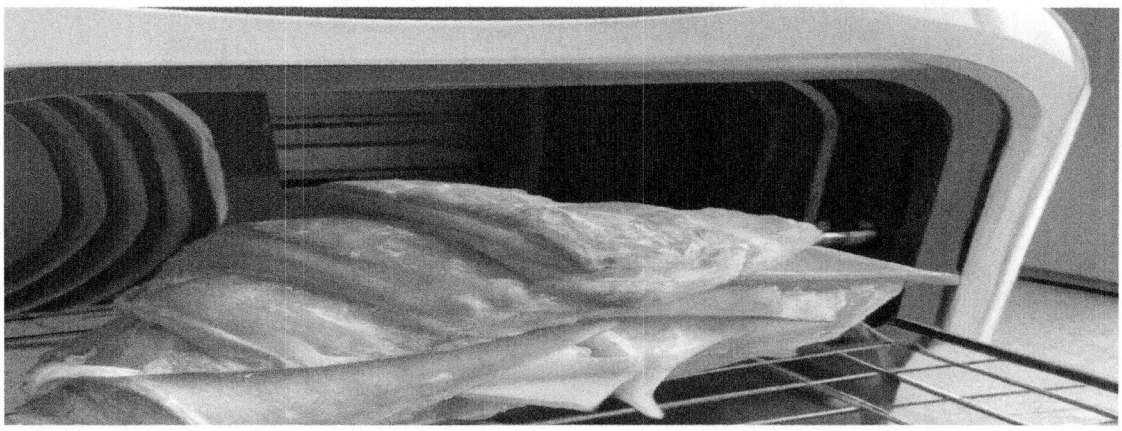

Ingredients

- 4 croissants, split open
- 8 slices of deli ham
- 8 slices of Swiss cheese
- 1/4 cup butter, melted
- 1 tsp Dijon mustard
- 1/4 tsp garlic powder
- Salt and pepper to taste

Instructions

1 Set the air fryer to a temperature of 400 degrees Fahrenheit.

2 Combine the melted butter, Dijon mustard, garlic powder, salt, and pepper in a small bowl.

3 Place the croissants on a cutting board, and brush the butter mixture on the inside of each croissant.

4 Place a slice of deli ham and a slice of Swiss cheese on the bottom half of each croissant.

5 Close the croissants and place them in the air fryer basket.

6 Cook for 8-10 minutes or until the croissants are golden brown and the cheese is melted.

7 Carefully remove the croissants from the air fryer and let them cool for a few minutes before serving.

Nutritional information per serving (based on 4 servings per recipe):

- Calories: 603
- Fat: 42g
- Carbohydrates: 30g
- Protein: 30g
- Sodium: 1272mg
- Cholesterol: 111mg

11. Air Fryer Breakfast Sandwich

Ingredients

- 4 English muffins, split and toasted
- 8 slices of cooked bacon
- 8 eggs
- 1/4 cup shredded cheddar cheese
- Salt and pepper to taste

Instructions

1. Set the air fryer to a temperature of 400 degrees Fahrenheit.
2. Crack the eggs into the air fryer basket, and season with salt and pepper.
3. Cook the eggs for 3-5 minutes or until the eggs are set but still moist.
4. Remove the eggs from the air fryer basket and set them aside.
5. On the bottom half of each toasted English muffin, place 2 slices of cooked bacon and 2 cooked eggs.
6. Add the shredded cheese on top of the eggs.
7. Place the sandwiches back into the air fryer basket and cook for an additional 2-3 minutes or until the cheese is melted.
8. Carefully remove the sandwiches from the air fryer and let them cool for a few minutes before serving.

Nutritional information per serving (based on 4 servings per recipe):

Calories: 704

Fat: 48g

Carbohydrates: 39g

Protein: 32g

Sodium: 1299mg

Cholesterol: 464mg

12. Air Fryer Breakfast Sausage

Ingredients

-1 lb breakfast sausage links or patties

Instructions

1 Set the air fryer to a temperature of 400 degrees Fahrenheit.

2 Place the breakfast sausage links or patties in the air fryer basket.

3 Cook for 8-10 minutes or until the sausage is browned and fully cooked.

4 Carefully remove the sausage from the air fryer and let cool for a few minutes before serving.

Nutritional information per serving (based on 4 servings per recipe, assuming 1 link per serving):

- Calories: 190

- Fat: 16g

- Carbohydrates: 1g

- Protein: 10g   - Sodium: 420mg   - Cholesterol: 45mg

13. Air Fryer Breakfast Scramble

Ingredients

-1 tbsp oil (such as olive or avocado)

-1/2 cup diced onion

-1/2 cup diced bell pepper

-1 cup diced mushrooms

-1 cup diced cooked breakfast sausage

-6 eggs

-1/4 cup milk

-1/4 cup shredded cheddar cheese

-Salt and pepper to taste

Instructions

1. Set the air fryer to a temperature of 400 degrees Fahrenheit.
2. In a skillet, heat the oil over medium flame Add the diced onion, bell pepper, mushrooms, and breakfast sausage. Cook for 5-7 minutes or until the vegetables are softened and the sausage is browned.
3. In a bowl, combine the eggs and milk. Stir with a whisk until blended. Add salt and pepper to taste.
4. Add the egg mixture to the skillet with the cooked vegetables and sausage. Stir the eggs occasionally while cooking them until they are set but still have a moist texture.
5. Carefully transfer the scramble to the air fryer basket.
6. Sprinkle shredded cheese over the top of the scramble.
7. Cook for an additional 2-3 minutes or until the cheese is melted.
8. Carefully remove the scramble from the air fryer and let cool for a few minutes before serving.

Nutritional information per serving (based on 4 servings per recipe):

Calories: 280

Fat: 21g

Carbohydrates: 4g

Protein: 18g

Sodium: 744mg

Cholesterol: 365mg

14. Air Fryer Breakfast Smoothie

Ingredients

- 1 banana
- 1 cup frozen berries (such as strawberries, blueberries, or raspberries)
- 1/2 cup Greek yogurt
- 1/2 cup orange juice
- 1 tbsp honey (optional)

Instructions

1. Put all of the ingredients into a blender and blend until they form a consistent mixture.
2. If the smoothie is too thick, add a little more orange juice or water.
3. Carefully pour the smoothie into a heat-proof container that fits in the air fryer basket.
4. Put all the items into a blender and mix until they are blended together smoothly.
5. Carefully remove the container from the air fryer and let cool for a few minutes before serving.

Nutritional information per serving (based on 4 servings per recipe):

Calories: 130

Fat: 1g

Carbohydrates: 27g

Protein: 6g

Sodium: 22mg

Cholesterol: 3mg

15. Air Fryer Breakfast Wrap

Ingredients

- Four flour tortillas
- 1/2 cup diced cooked breakfast sausage
- 1/2 cup diced potatoes
- 1/2 cup diced bell pepper
- 1/4 cup diced onion
- 4 eggs
- 1/4 cup shredded cheddar cheese
- Salt and pepper to taste

Instructions

1. Set the air fryer to a temperature of 400 degrees Fahrenheit.
2. In a skillet, cook the diced breakfast sausage, diced potatoes, diced bell pepper, and diced onion over medium heat until the vegetables are softened and the sausage is browned.
3. Crack the eggs into the skillet, and scramble with the sausage and vegetables. Season with salt and pepper.
4. Place 1/4 of the sausage and egg mixture on one-half of each tortilla.
5. Stir in the shredded cheese to combine it with the mixture.
6. Fold the other half of the tortilla over the filling, creating a wrap.
7. Place the wraps in the air fryer basket.
8. Cook for 8-10 minutes or until the wraps are golden brown and the cheese is melted.
9. Carefully remove the wraps from the air fryer and let them cool for a few minutes before serving.

Nutritional information per serving (based on 4 servings per recipe):

Calories: 354

Fat: 21g

Carbohydrates: 22g

Protein: 16g

Sodium: 637mg

Cholesterol: 212mg

16. Air Fryer Breakfast Quinoa

Ingredients

- 1 cup of rinsed and drained quinoa
- 2 cups water or low-sodium chicken broth
- 1 teaspoon olive oil
- 1/4 teaspoon salt
- 1/4 cup diced onion
- One-fourth cup of diced red bell pepper.
- 1/4 cup diced green bell pepper
- 1/4 cup diced tomatoes
- 1/4 cup diced avocado
- 1/4 cup crumbled feta cheese
- 2 tablespoons of finely chopped cilantro

Instructions

1. In a medium saucepan, combine the quinoa, water or broth, olive oil, and salt. Bring to a boil over high heat.
2. Reduce the heat to low and cover. Simmer for 18-20 minutes, or until the quinoa is tender and the water is absorbed. Remove from heat and fluff with a fork.
3. Set the air fryer to 375 degrees F before using.
4. In a medium bowl, combine the quinoa, onion, bell peppers, tomatoes, avocado, feta cheese, and cilantro. Toss to combine.
5. Place the quinoa mixture in the air fryer basket and cook for 8-10 minutes, or until the quinoa is heated through and the vegetables are tender.
6. Serve warm, garnished with additional cilantro, if desired.

Nutritional information (per serving):

Calories: 250, Fat: 12g, Saturated Fat: 4g, Cholesterol: 20mg, Sodium: 220mg, Carbohydrates: 27g, Fiber: 3g, Sugar: 2g, Protein: 9g.

17. Air Fryer Breakfast Yogurt

Ingredients

- 2 cups Greek yogurt
- 1/4 cup honey
- 1 teaspoon vanilla extract
- 1/4 teaspoon ground cinnamon
- 1/4 cup granola
- 1/4 cup fresh berries (optional)

Instructions

1. In a medium bowl, combine Greek yogurt, honey, vanilla extract, and cinnamon.
2. Set the air fryer to a temperature of 350 degrees Fahrenheit.
3. Pour the yogurt mixture into a greased air fryer-safe dish.
4. Place the dish in the air fryer and cook for 10-15 minutes or until the yogurt is set.
5. Remove the dish from the air fryer and let it cool for a few minutes.
6. Once cooled add granola and fresh berries (if desired) on top of the yogurt.
7. Serve and enjoy

Nutritional information (per serving):

Calories: 250, Fat: 5g, Saturated Fat: 3g, Cholesterol: 15mg, Sodium: 65mg, Carbohydrates: 32g, Fiber: 1g, Sugar: 27g, Protein: 16g.

18. Air Fryer Breakfast Omelette

Ingredients

- 4 large eggs
- 1/4 cup milk
- Salt and pepper, to taste
- 1/4 cup diced ham
- 1/4 cup diced bell peppers
- 1/4 cup diced onion
- 1/4 cup shredded cheddar cheese

Instructions

1. Mix the eggs, milk, salt, and pepper together in a medium bowl using a whisk.
2. Stir in the diced ham, bell peppers, and onion.
3. Set the air fryer to 350 degrees Fahrenheit, then grease the basket with cooking spray. Afterward, pour the egg mixture into the air fryer basket.
4. Bake in the oven for 8-10 minutes or until the eggs are firm and the cheese has melted.
5. Carefully remove the omelette from the air fryer using a spatula.
6. Slice and serve warm.

Nutritional information (per serving):

Calories: 190, Fat: 12g, Saturated Fat: 5g, Cholesterol: 290mg, Sodium: 470mg, Carbohydrates: 3g, Fiber: 0g, Sugar: 2g, Protein: 16g.

19. Air Fryer Breakfast Frittata

Ingredients

- 1 tablespoon olive oil
- 1/4 cup diced onion
- 1/4 cup diced bell pepper
- 1/4 cup diced mushrooms
- 6 large eggs
- 1/4 cup milk
- Salt and pepper, to taste
- 1/4 cup shredded cheddar cheese

Instructions

1. Mix the eggs, milk, salt, and pepper together in a medium bowl using a whisk.
2. Stir in the diced ham, bell peppers, and onion.
3. Set the air fryer to 350 degrees Fahrenheit, then grease the basket with cooking spray. Afterward, pour the egg mixture into the air fryer basket.
4. Bake in the oven for 8-10 minutes or until the eggs are firm and the cheese has melted.
5. Carefully remove the omelette from the air fryer using a spatula.
6. Slice and serve warm.

Nutritional information (per serving):

Calories: 190, Fat: 12g, Saturated Fat: 5g, Cholesterol: 290mg, Sodium: 470mg, Carbohydrates: 3g, Fiber: 0g, Sugar: 2g, Protein: 16g.

20. Air Fryer Breakfast Crepes

Ingredients

- 1 cup all-purpose flour
- 2 eggs
- 1/2 cup milk
- 1/2 cup water
- 2 tablespoons melted butter
- 1/4 teaspoon salt
- 1/4 cup diced ham
- 1/4 cup diced mushrooms
- 1/4 cup diced bell pepper
- 1/4 cup shredded cheese
- 1/4 cup diced tomatoes

Instructions

1. In a large mixing bowl, whisk together the flour, eggs, milk, water, melted butter, and salt until smooth.
2. Heat the air fryer to 350F.
3. Take a small amount of batter and pour it into the air fryer basket, tilting the basket to spread the batter evenly across the bottom.
4. Cook the ingredients for 2-3 minutes, or until the edges turn a golden brown color.
5. Carefully remove the crepe from the air fryer and place it on a plate.
6. For the rest of the batter, repeat the same steps.
7. Once all crepes are ready, place some diced ham, mushrooms, bell pepper, shredded cheese, and diced tomatoes on one half of the crepe and fold the other half over it.
8. Return the filled crepes to the air fryer and cook for an additional 2-3 minutes, until the cheese is melted and the crepes are heated through.
9. Remove the crepes from the air fryer and serve warm.

Nutritional information (per serving):

Calories: 250, Fat: 13g, Saturated Fat: 6g, Cholesterol: 95mg, Sodium: 440mg, Carbohydrates: 23g, Fiber: 1g, Sugar: 2g, Protein: 10g.

21. Air Fryer Breakfast Waffles

Ingredients

- 1 1/2 cups all-purpose flour

- 2 teaspoons baking powder

- 1/4 teaspoon salt

- 1 egg

- 1 cup milk

- 2 tablespoons melted butter

- 1 teaspoon vanilla extract

-Maple syrup and butter, for serving (optional)

Instructions

1. In a large bowl, whisk together the flour, baking powder, and salt.
2. In a different bowl, combine the egg, milk, melted butter, and vanilla extract, stirring them together with a whisk.
3. Combine the wet ingredients with the dry ingredients, stirring until just blended.
4. Preheat the air fryer to 375F.
5. Add the wet ingredients to the dry ingredients and stir until everything is evenly blended.
6. Cook for 8-10 minutes, or until the waffles are golden brown and crispy.
7. Carefully remove the waffles from the air fryer and place them on a plate.
8. For the rest of the batter, repeat the same steps.
9. Serve the waffles warm with butter and maple syrup, if desired.

Nutritional information (per serving):

Calories: 250, Fat: 12g, Saturated Fat: 7g, Cholesterol: 55mg, Sodium: 240mg, Carbohydrates: 30g, Fiber: 1g, Sugar: 4g, Protein: 5g.

22. Air Fryer Breakfast Pancakes

Ingredients

- 1 cup all-purpose flour
- 2 tablespoons sugar
- 2 teaspoons baking powder
- 1/2 teaspoon salt
- 1 egg
- 1 cup milk
- 2 tablespoons melted butter
- 1 teaspoon vanilla extract
- Maple syrup and butter, for serving (optional)

Instructions

1. In a mixing bowl, combine the flour, sugar, baking powder, and salt, and whisk them together.
2. In a separate mixing bowl, whisk together the egg, milk, melted butter, and vanilla extract.
3. Add the wet ingredients to the dry ingredients and combine until blended.
4. reheat the air fryer to 375F.
5. Using a ladle or measuring cup, pour the pancake batter into the preheated air fryer, spreading it evenly across the bottom of the basket.
6. Cook for 4-5 minutes or until the pancakes are golden brown and cooked through.
7. Carefully remove the pancakes from the air fryer and place them on a plate.
8. Repeat these steps again with the remaining batter.
9. Serve the pancakes warm with butter and maple syrup, if desired.

Nutritional information (per serving):

Calories: 250, Fat: 11g, Saturated Fat: 6g, Cholesterol: 55mg, Sodium: 340mg, Carbohydrates: 29g, Fiber: 1g, Sugar: 10g, Protein: 5g.

23. Air Fryer Breakfast Strata

Ingredients

- 8 slices of bread, cut into cubes

- 1 cup diced cooked ham

- 1 cup diced cooked bacon

- 1 cup shredded cheddar cheese

- 1/2 cup diced onion

- 1/2 cup diced bell pepper

- 8 eggs

- 1 1/2 cups milk

- 1/4 teaspoon salt

- 1/4 teaspoon black pepper

- 1/4 teaspoon dried thyme (optional)

Instructions

1. Preheat the air fryer to 350F.
2. In a large mixing bowl, combine the bread cubes, diced ham, bacon, cheese, onion, and bell pepper.
3. In a separate mixing bowl, whisk together the eggs, milk, salt, pepper, and dried thyme (if using).
4. Spread the egg mixture over the bread cubes, ensuring that each piece is evenly covered.
5. Spray the air fryer basket with cooking spray to lubricate it.
6. Gently pour the egg mixture over the bread cubes, making sure each one is evenly coated. Gently pour the egg mixture over the bread cubes, making sure each one is evenly coated.
7. Cook for 20-25 minutes, or until the eggs are set and the top is golden brown.
8. Carefully remove the strata from the air fryer and let it cool for a few minutes before slicing.
9. Serve warm.

Nutritional information (per serving):

Calories: 400, Fat: 25g, Saturated Fat: 11g, Cholesterol: 245mg, Sodium: 1050mg, Carbohydrates: 25g, Fiber: 2g, Sugar: 6g, Protein: 23g.

24. Air Fryer Breakfast Biscuit

Ingredients

- 2 cups of all-purpose flour and 1/2 teaspoon of salt.

- 1/4 cup cold butter, cut into small pieces

- 1 tablespoon baking powder

- 3/4 cup milk

Instructions

1. In a large bowl, combine the flour, baking powder, and salt together using a whisk.
2. Using a pastry cutter or your fingers, cut the butter into the flour mixture until it resembles coarse crumbs.
3. Slowly add the milk to the mixture, stirring until the dough comes together.
4. Preheat the air fryer to 375F.
5. Coat the air fryer basket with a thin layer of cooking oil using a spray bottle.
6. Scoop the dough using a cookie scoop or spoon onto the air fryer basket.
7. Bake the biscuits for 8-10 minutes, or until they are a golden brown color and fully cooked.
8. Carefully remove the biscuits from the air fryer and let them cool for a few minutes before serving.
9. You can enjoy this dish with butter, jelly, or honey.

Nutritional information (per serving):

Calories: 200, Fat: 9g, Saturated Fat: 5g, Cholesterol: 20mg, Sodium: 310mg, Carbohydrates: 25g, Fiber: 1g, Sugar: 2g, Protein: 3g.

25. Air Fryer Breakfast Hash

Ingredients

- 1 tablespoon olive oil
- 1/2 cup diced onion
- 1/2 cup diced bell pepper
- 1/2 cup diced cooked potatoes
- 1/2 cup diced cooked ham
- 1/4 teaspoon salt
- 1/4 teaspoon black pepper
- 4 eggs

Instructions

1. Preheat the air fryer to 375F.
2. In a skillet, heat the olive oil over medium heat. Add the onion, bell pepper, potatoes, ham, salt, and pepper, and sauté for 5-7 minutes, or until the vegetables are tender.
3. Spray the air fryer basket with cooking spray to lubricate it.
4. Place the skillet contents into the air fryer basket.
5. Crack the eggs over the top of the hash.
6. Cook for 8-10 minutes, or until the eggs are cooked to your preference.
7. Carefully remove the hash from the air fryer and serve warm.
8. You can also add some shredded cheese on top before the last minutes of cooking.

Nutritional information (per serving):

Calories: 280, Fat: 17g, Saturated Fat: 4g, Cholesterol: 195mg, Sodium: 520mg, Carbohydrates: 17g, Fiber: 2g, Sugar: 3g, Protein: 14g.

26. Air Fryer Breakfast Croquette

Ingredients

- 2 cups cooked and mashed potatoes
- 1/2 cup diced cooked bacon
- 1/4 cup diced onion
- 1/4 cup grated cheddar cheese
- 1 egg
- 1/4 cup all-purpose flour
- 1/4 cup breadcrumbs
- Salt and pepper, to taste
- Oil for spraying

Instructions

1. In a large bowl, mix together the mashed potatoes, bacon, onion, cheese, egg, flour, breadcrumbs, salt, and pepper until evenly combined.
2. sing your hands, shape the mixture into small, oval-shaped croquettes.
3. Preheat the air fryer to 375F.
4. Grease the air fryer basket with oil spray.
5. Place the croquettes in the air fryer basket, making sure they aren't touching.
6. Cook for 8-10 minutes or until golden brown and crispy.
7. Carefully remove the croquettes from the air fryer and place them on a plate.
8. Serve the croquettes warm with your favorite dipping sauce.

Nutritional information (per serving):

Calories: 200, Fat: 8g, Saturated Fat: 3g, Cholesterol: 55mg, Sodium: 400mg, Carbohydrates: 22g, Fiber: 2g, Sugar: 1g, Protein: 7g.

27. Air Fryer Breakfast Churro

Ingredients

- 1 cup water
- /2 cup unsalted butter
- 1/4 teaspoon salt
- 1 cup all-purpose flour
- 3 large eggs
- 1/4 cup granulated sugar
- 1 teaspoon ground cinnamon
- Oil for spraying

Instructions

1. In a medium saucepan, mix together the water, butter, and salt. Bring to a boil over medium heat.
2. Remove the saucepan from the heat and add the flour all at once, stirring quickly with a wooden spoon until the dough comes together.
3. Return the saucepan to low heat and stir the dough for an additional 2-3 minutes, until it forms a ball and pulls away from the sides of the pan.
4. Take the dough off the heat and let it cool down for a few minutes.
5. After cooling, mix in the eggs one at a time, stirring well after each one.
6. Preheat the air fryer to 400F.
7. Spray the air fryer basket with oil to lubricate it.
8. Using a piping bag or a plastic bag with the corner cut off, pipe the dough into the air fryer basket in the shape of churros.
9. Mix together sugar and cinnamon in a small bowl.
10. Once the churros are cooked and golden brown, remove them from the air fryer and roll them in the cinnamon-sugar mixture.
11. 1Serve the churros warm with your favorite dipping sauce.

Nutritional information (per serving):

Calories: 200, Fat: 13g, Saturated Fat: 7g, Cholesterol: 85mg, Sodium: 120mg, Carbohydrates: 17g, Fiber: 0g, Sugar: 6g, Protein: 3g.

28. Air Fryer Breakfast Muffin

Ingredients

- 1 1/2 cups all-purpose flour
- 1/2 cup granulated sugar
- 1 teaspoon baking powder
- 1/4 teaspoon salt
- 1/2 cup milk
- 1/4 cup vegetable oil
- 1 egg
- 1 teaspoon vanilla extract
- 1 cup fresh or frozen berries (optional)

Instructions

1. In a large bowl, combine the flour, sugar, baking powder, and salt using a whisk.
2. In a separate mixing bowl, whisk together the milk, oil, egg, and vanilla extract.
3. Empty the wet ingredients into the dry ingredients and stir until blended. If you are using berries, gently fold them into the batter.
4. Preheat the air fryer to 375F.
5. Spray the air fryer basket with cooking oil to grease it.
6. Using a cookie scoop or spoon, scoop the muffin batter into the air fryer basket.
7. Cook for 12-15 minutes, or until the muffins are golden brown and cooked through.
8. Carefully remove the muffins from the air fryer and let them cool for a few minutes before serving.
9. Serve the muffins warm or at room temperature.

Nutritional information (per serving):

Calories: 200, Fat: 8g, Saturated Fat: 5g, Cholesterol: 20mg, Sodium: 160mg, Carbohydrates: 27g,

29. Air Fryer Breakfast Scones

Ingredients

- In a bowl, mix together 2 cups of all-purpose flour, 1/4 cup of granulated sugar, 2 teaspoons of baking powder, and 1/4 teaspoon of salt.
- 1/2 cup cold butter, cut into small pieces
- 1/2 cup heavy cream
- 1 egg
- 1 teaspoon vanilla extract
- 1/2 cup dried fruit or berries (optional

Instructions

1. In a large mixing bowl, whisk together the flour, sugar, baking powder, and salt.
2. Using either a pastry cutter or your fingers, mix the butter into the flour until it looks like coarse crumbs.
3. In a different bowl, use a whisk to combine the cream, egg, and vanilla extract.
4. If you are using dried fruit or berries, gently fold them into the wet ingredients.
5. Add the wet components to the dry ones and blend until they are thoroughly incorporated.
6. Preheat the air fryer to 375F.
7. Spray cooking spray onto the air fryer basket to grease it.
8. Using your hands, shape the dough into a circle about 1 inch thick. Cut the circle into 8 wedges.
9. Place the scones in the preheated air fryer basket, making sure they aren't touching.
10. Cook for 12-15 minutes or until golden brown.
11. Carefully remove the scones from the air fryer and let them cool for a few minutes before serving.
12. Serve the scones warm or at room temperature, with butter or jam if desired.

Nutritional information (per serving):

Calories: 280, Fat: 18g, Saturated Fat: 11g, Cholesterol: 75mg, Sodium: 300mg, Carbohydrates: 26g, Fiber: 1g, Sugar: 8g, Protein: 3g.

30. Air Fryer Breakfast Parfait

Ingredients

- 1 cup of non-fat Greek yogurt
- 1/4 cup unsweetened almond milk
- 1 tablespoon honey
- 1/2 teaspoon vanilla extract
- 1/2 cup fresh berries (blueberries, raspberries, strawberries, etc)
- 1/4 cup rolled oats
- 2 tablespoons chopped nuts (walnuts, almonds, pecans, etc)

Instructions

1. In a small bowl, combine the Greek yogurt, almond milk, honey, and vanilla extract, whisking them together.
2. Preheat the air fryer to 350F.
3. In a heatproof bowl or jar that will fit in your air fryer, layer the yogurt mixture, berries, oats, and nuts. Repeat until you reach the top of the container.
4. Place the bowl in the air fryer and cook for about 15 minutes, or until the oats are lightly toasted and the nuts are slightly golden brown.
5. Carefully remove the parfait from the air fryer and let it cool for a few minutes before serving.
6. Serve the parfait chilled.

Nutritional information:

Calories: 200, Fat: 7g, Saturated Fat: 1g, Cholesterol: 5mg, Sodium: 60mg, Carbohydrates: 25g, Fiber: 4g, Sugar: 14g, Protein: 9g.

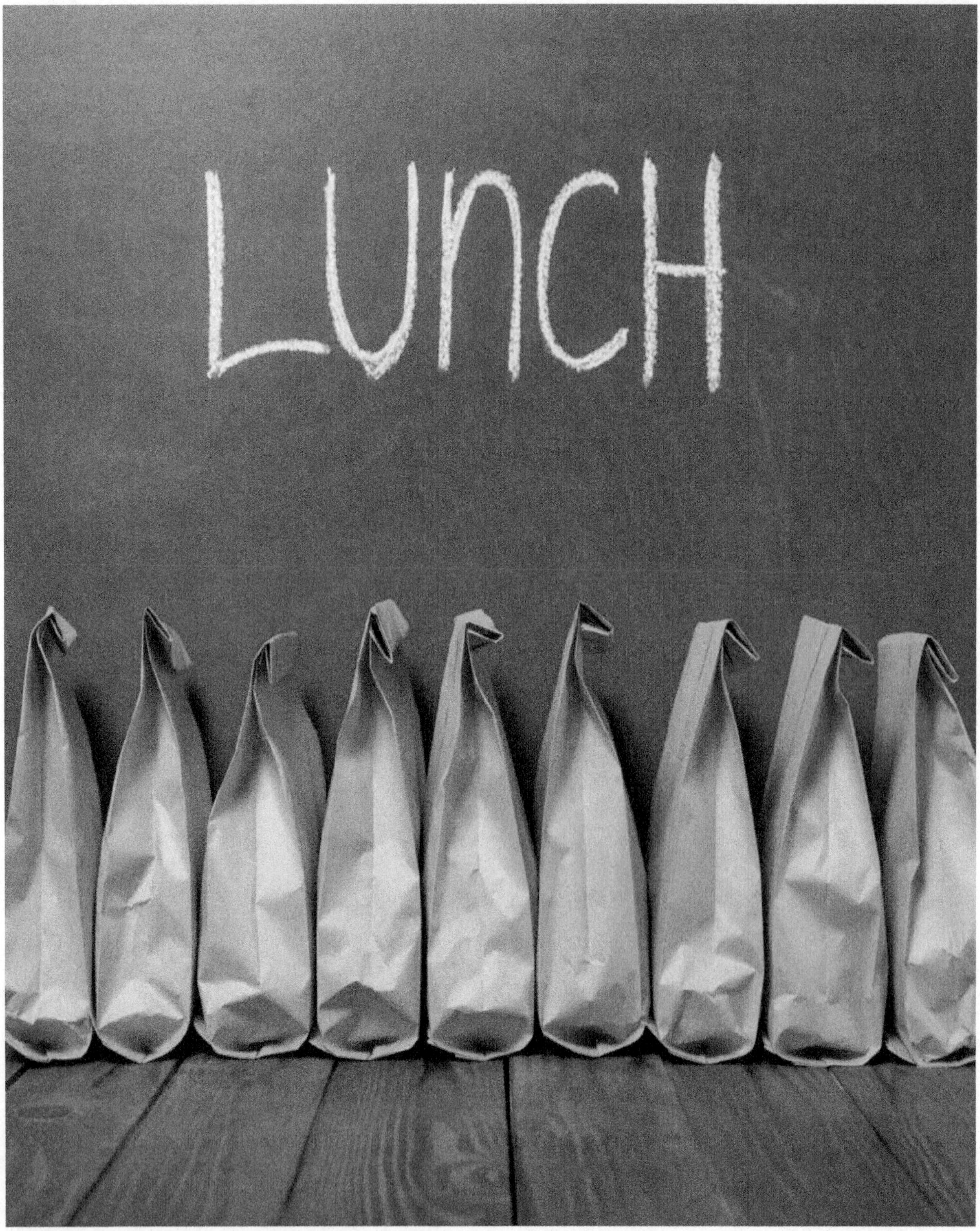
LUNCH

LUNCH

1. Air Fryer Baked Potatoes

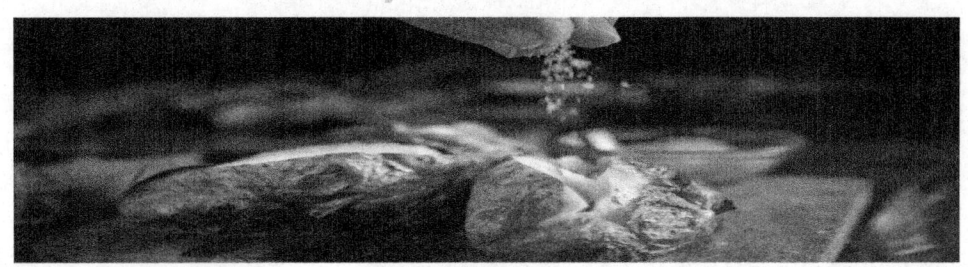

Ingredients

- 4 medium-sized russet potatoes
- 1 tsp olive oil
- Salt and pepper, to taste

Instructions

1. Wash and dry the potatoes, then poke them several times with a fork.
2. Season each potato with salt and pepper after brushing it with olive oil.
3. Place the potatoes in the air fryer and cook at 400 degrees F for 25-30 minutes, or until the potatoes are fork-tender.
4. Remove from the air fryer and let cool for a few minutes before slicing and serving.

Nutritional Information (per potato):

-Calories: 130

-Fat: 0.4g

-Saturated Fat: 0.1g

-Cholesterol: 0mg

-Sodium: 9mg

-Carbohydrates: 29g

-Fiber: 2g

-Sugar: 1g

-Protein: 2g

2. Air Fryer Chicken Fajitas

Ingredients

- 1 lb boneless, skinless chicken breasts, sliced into thin strips
- 1 red bell pepper, sliced
- 1 green bell pepper, sliced
- 1 onion, sliced
- 1 tbsp olive oil
- 1 tsp chili powder
- 1 tsp cumin
- 1/2 tsp garlic powder
- Salt and pepper, to taste
- 8 small whole wheat tortillas

Instructions

1. In a large bowl, combine the sliced chicken, bell peppers, onion, olive oil, chili powder, cumin, garlic powder, salt, and pepper. Toss to coat the vegetables and chicken evenly.
2. Place the chicken and vegetables in the air fryer basket and cook at 400 degrees F for 12-15 minutes, or until the chicken is cooked through and the vegetables are tender-crisp.
3. Remove from the air fryer and let cool for a few minutes before filling the tortillas with the chicken and vegetables.
4. Roll up the tortillas and serve.

Nutritional Information (per serving, 2 fajitas):

-Calories: 259

-Fat: 8g

-Saturated Fat: 2g

-Cholesterol: 72mg

-Sodium: 222mg

-Carbohydrates: 23g

-Fiber: 4g

-Sugar: 3g

-Protein: 24g

3. Air Fryer Eggplant Parmesan

Ingredients

- 1 large eggplant, sliced into 1/4-inch rounds
- 1 cup all-purpose flour
- 2 eggs, beaten
- 1 cup breadcrumbs
- 1/2 cup grated Parmesan cheese
- 1 tsp dried basil
- 1 cup of shredded mozzarella cheese
- 1 tsp dried oregano
- Salt and pepper, to taste
- 1 cup marinara sauce

Instructions

1. Set up a breading station by placing flour in one shallow dish, beaten eggs in another, and breadcrumbs mixed with Parmesan cheese, basil, oregano, salt, and pepper in a third dish.
2. put each eggplant slice in flour, shaking off any excess, dip in the beaten eggs, and coat in the breadcrumb mixture.
3. lace the breaded eggplant slices in the air fryer basket and cook at 400 degrees F for 10-12 minutes until golden brown and crispy.
4. Remove from the air fryer and let cool for a few minutes.
5. Preheat oven to 350F.
6. The bottom of a baking dish should be covered with marinara sauce. Layer eggplant slices on top of the sauce.
7. Sprinkle shredded mozzarella cheese over the eggplant.
8. Bake in the preheated oven for 20-25 minutes, or until the cheese is melted and bubbly.

Nutritional Information (per serving, 1/4 of the recipe):

-Calories: 230

-Fat: 12g

-Saturated Fat: 5g

-Cholesterol: 80mg

-Sodium: 635mg

-Carbohydrates: 19g

- Fiber: 4   -Sugar: 7g-Protein: 12g

4. Air Fryer Grilled Cheese Sandwich

Ingredients

- 2 tbsp reduced-fat butter, divided
- 2 slices whole wheat bread
- 2 slices low-fat cheddar cheese

Instructions

1. Each piece of bread should have 1 tbsp of butter spread on one side.
2. Place cheese in between the slices of bread, butter side out.
3. Place the sandwich in the air fryer and cook at 400 degrees F for 3-5 minutes, or until the bread is golden brown and the cheese is melted.
4. Remove from the air fryer and let cool for a few minutes before slicing and serving.

Nutritional Information (per serving, 1 sandwich):

-Calories: 250

-Fat: 14g

-Saturated Fat: 8g

-Cholesterol: 35mg

-Sodium: 550mg

-Carbohydrates: 24g

-Fiber: 3g

-Sugar: 4g

-Protein: 12g

5. Air Fryer Grilled Vegetable Skewers

Ingredients

- 1 red bell pepper, sliced
- 1 green bell pepper, sliced
- 1 onion, sliced
- 1 zucchini, sliced
- 1 yellow squash, sliced
- 1/4 cup olive oil
- 2 cloves garlic, minced
- 1 tsp dried basil
- 1 tsp dried oregano
- Salt and pepper, to taste

Instructions

1. 400°F should be the air fryer's set temperature.
2. Thread the bell peppers, onion, zucchini, and yellow squash onto skewers.
3. In a small bowl, mix together olive oil, minced garlic, basil, oregano, salt, and pepper.
4. Apply the olive oil mixture on the skewers.
5. Place skewers in the air fryer and cook for 10-15 minutes, or until vegetables are tender and slightly charred, turning the skewers occasionally.
6. Before serving, take the food out of the air fryer and let it cool for a while.

Nutritional Information (per serving, 2 skewers)

-Calories: 200

-Fat: 18g

-Saturated Fat: 2.5g

-Cholesterol: 0mg

-Sodium: 5mg

-Carbohydrates: 8g

-Fiber: 2g

-Sugar: 4g

-Protein: 2g

6. Air Fryer Roasted Asparagus

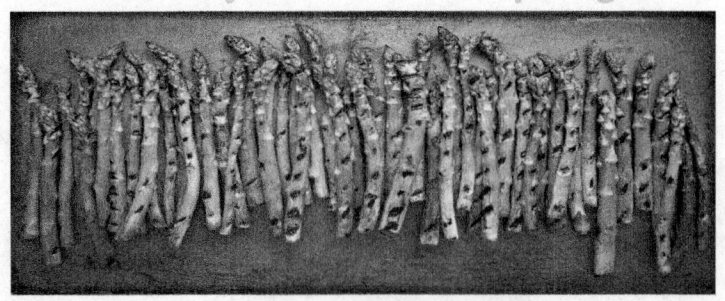

Ingredients

- 1 lb asparagus, trimmed
- 1 tbsp olive oil
- Salt and pepper, to taste

Instructions

1. 400°F should be the air fryer's set temperature.
2. Place asparagus in a large bowl and toss with olive oil, salt, and pepper.
3. Place asparagus in the air fryer and cook for 8-10 minutes, or until tender and slightly charred, shaking the basket occasionally.
4. Before serving, take the food out of the air fryer and let it cool for a while.

Nutritional Information (per serving, 1/4 lb of asparagus)

-Calories: 40

-Fat: 3.5g

-Saturated Fat: 0.5g

-Cholesterol: 0mg

-Sodium: 3mg

-Carbohydrates: 3g

-Fiber: 2g

-Sugar: 2g

-Protein: 2g

7. Air Fryer Salmon Cakes

Ingredients

- 1 lb skinless salmon fillet, cooked and flaked
- 1/4 cup diced onion
- 1/4 cup diced celery
- 1/4 cup diced red bell pepper
- 1 egg, lightly beaten
- 2 tbsp reduced-fat mayonnaise
- 1 tbsp Dijon mustard
- 1 tbsp lemon juice
- 1/4 cup whole wheat breadcrumbs
- Salt and pepper, to taste

Instructions

1. In a medium bowl, combine the flaked salmon, onion, celery, red bell pepper, egg, mayonnaise, Dijon mustard, lemon juice, breadcrumbs, salt, and pepper. Mix well.
2. Form mixture into 8 patties.
3. 400°F should be the air fryer's set temperature.
4. Place the patties in the air fryer basket and cook for 6-8 minutes, or until golden brown and cooked through, flipping halfway through.
5. Remove from the air fryer and let cool for a few minutes before serving.

Nutritional Information (per serving, 2 cakes)

-Calories: 260

-Fat: 14g

-Saturated Fat: 2g

-Cholesterol: 75mg

-Sodium: 540mg

-Carbohydrates: 12g

-Fiber: 2g

-Sugar: 2g

-Protein: 24g

8. Air Fryer Shrimp Tacos

Ingredients

- 1 lb raw shrimp, peeled and deveined
- 2 tbsp olive oil
- 2 cloves garlic, minced
- 1 tsp chili powder
- 1 tsp paprika
- 1 tsp cumin
- Salt and pepper, to taste
- 8 small corn tortillas
- 1/2 cup shredded red cabbage
- 1/4 cup diced red onion
- 2 tbsp chopped cilantro
- 2 tbsp sour cream
- 1 lime, cut into wedges

Instructions

1. Mix together the shrimp, olive oil, garlic, chili powder, paprika, cumin, salt, and pepper in a large bowl.
2. Place the shrimp in the air fryer and cook at 400 degrees F for 5-7 minutes, or until the shrimp are pink and cooked through.
3. Remove from the air fryer and let cool for a few minutes before assembling the tacos.
4. Heat the tortillas in the air fryer for about 30 seconds each or until warm and pliable.
5. Assemble the tacos by placing some cooked shrimp, shredded cabbage, red onion, cilantro, and a dollop of sour cream in each tortilla.
6. Serve with lime wedges on the side.

Nutritional Information (per serving, 2 tacos)

-Calories: 260

-Fat: 12g

-Saturated Fat: 2g

-Cholesterol: 145mg

-Sodium: 310mg

-Carbohydrates: 20g

-Fiber: 2g

-Sugar: 2g

-Protein: 18g

9. Air Fryer Spinach and Cheese Frittata

Ingredients

- 8 eggs

- 1/2 cup milk

- 1/2 cup of grated Parmesan cheese

- Salt and pepper, to taste

- 1 tbsp olive oil

- 1 small onion, diced

- 2 cloves garlic, minced

- 2 cups freshly cleaned and sliced spinach

- Half a cup of shredded mozzarella cheese

Instructions

1. In a large bowl, stir together the milk, eggs, salt, and pepper.
2. The air fryer should be preheated to 350 degrees F.
3. Olive oil should be heated in a pan over medium heat. Cook the onion and garlic for approximately 5 minutes, or until tender.
4. Add the spinach to the skillet and cook until wilted, about 3 minutes.
5. Stir in the spinach mixture and cheese into the egg mixture.
6. Grease the air fryer-safe dish with some oil, pour in the mixture and place the dish in the air fryer.
7. Cook the frittata for 18-20 minutes or until set.
8. Remove from the air fryer and let cool for a few minutes before slicing and serving.

Nutritional Information (per serving, 1 slice)

-Calories: 200

-Fat: 14g

-Saturated Fat: 6g

-Cholesterol: 190mg

-Sodium: 350mg

-Carbohydrates: 4g

-Fiber: 1g

-Sugar: 2g

-Protein: 14g

10. Air Fryer Steak Fries

Ingredients

- 2 large russet potatoes, washed and sliced into wedges
- 2 tbsp olive oil
- Salt and pepper, to taste

Instructions

1. The air fryer should be set at 400 degrees F.
2. Put the potato wedges in a big basin and add the olive oil, salt, and pepper.
3. Place the wedges in the air fryer in a single layer and cook for 15-20 minutes, or until golden brown and crispy, flipping halfway through.
4. Remove from the air fryer and let cool for a few minutes before serving.

Nutritional Information (per serving, 1/4 of the recipe)

-Calories: 150

-Fat: 7g

-Saturated Fat: 1g

-Cholesterol: 0mg

-Sodium: 10mg

-Carbohydrates: 21g

-Fiber: 2g

-Sugar: 1g

- Protein: 2g

11. Avocado and Egg Salad

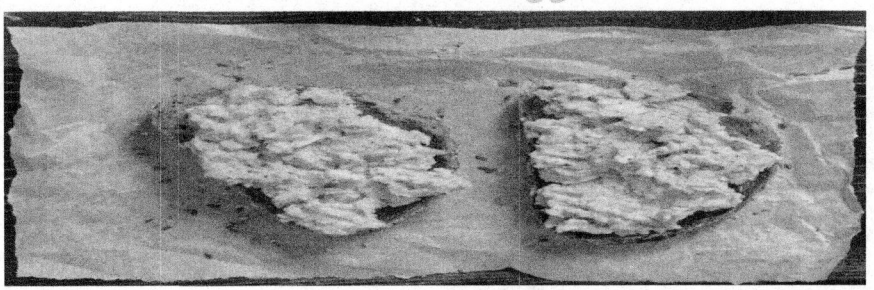

Ingredients

- Three peeled and chopped hard-boiled eggs
- 1 ripe avocado, peeled and diced
- 2 tbsp chopped red onion
- 2 tbsp chopped cilantro
- 2 tbsp plain Greek yogurt
- 1 tbsp mayonnaise
- 1 tbsp fresh lime juice
- Salt and pepper, to taste
- Lettuce leaves or whole wheat bread for serving (optional)

Instructions

1. Combine the diced eggs, avocado, red onion, and cilantro in a medium bowl.
2. In a small bowl, mix together the Greek yogurt, mayonnaise, lime juice, salt, and pepper.
3. Stir the dressing into the egg mixture.
4. Store the container in the refrigerator for a minimum of 30 minutes.
5. Serve on top of lettuce leaves or whole wheat bread if desired.

Nutritional Information (per serving, 1/4 of the recipe)

-Calories: 210

-Fat: 18g

-Saturated Fat: 4g

-Cholesterol: 185mg

-Sodium: 170mg

-Carbohydrates: 8g

-Fiber: 4g

-Sugar: 2g

-Protein: 7g

12. Baked Apple Chips

Ingredients

- 2 large apples, cored and thinly sliced
- 1 tsp ground cinnamon
- 1/4 tsp ground nutmeg
- 1/4 tsp salt

Instructions

1. Preheat the oven to 200 degrees F (95 degrees C) and line a baking sheet with parchment paper.
2. On the baking sheet that has been prepared, arrange the apple slices in a single layer.
3. In a small bowl, mix together the cinnamon, nutmeg, and salt. Spread the mixture over the apples. Bake the apples in the preheated oven for 1 hour and 30 minutes, or until they are dry and crispy.
4. Before serving, take the dish out of the air fryer and let it cool for a while.

Nutritional Information (per serving, 1/4 of recipe)

-Calories: 40

-Fat: 0g

-Saturated Fat: 0g

-Cholesterol: 0mg

-Sodium: 45mg

-Carbohydrates: 11g

-Fiber: 2g

-Sugar: 9g

-Protein: 0g

13. Baked Sweet Potato Fries

Ingredients

- 2 large sweet potatoes, peeled and cut into wedges
- 1 tbsp olive oil
- Salt and pepper, to taste

Instructions

1. Set the oven to 220 degrees Celsius.
2. In a large bowl, mix the sweet potato wedges with olive oil, salt, and pepper.
3. Place the wedges on a baking sheet and bake for 20-25 minutes or until golden brown and crispy, flipping them halfway through.
4. Before serving, take the dish out of the air fryer and let it cool for a while.

Nutritional Information (per serving, 1/4 of the recipe)

-Calories: 120

-Fat: 4g

-Saturated Fat: 0.5g

-Cholesterol: 0mg

-Sodium: 65mg

-Carbohydrates: 21g

-Fiber: 3g

-Sugar: 5g

-Protein: 2g

14. Broccoli and Cheese Stuffed Portobellos

Ingredients

- 4 large portobello mushroom caps, cleaned and stems removed
- 1 tbsp olive oil
- Salt and pepper, to taste
- 2 cups broccoli florets
- 1/4 cup diced onion
- 2 cloves garlic, minced
- 1/2 cup shredded cheddar cheese
- 1/4 cup grated Parmesan cheese
- 2 eggs, lightly beaten

Instructions

1. The oven's temperature should be set to 375 degrees.
2. Season the mushroom caps with salt and pepper after brushing them with olive oil.
3. Place the mushroom caps on a baking sheet, gill side up.
4. In a skillet, heat the olive oil over medium heat. Cook the onion and garlic for approximately 5 minutes, or until tender.
5. Add the broccoli florets and cook for an additional 5 minutes or until tender.
6. Remove from the heat and set it aside for a few minutes to cool.
7. Mix in the cheese, and eggs and spoon the mixture into the mushroom caps.
8. Bake the mushrooms in the preheated oven for 20-25 minutes or until the mushrooms are tender and the filling is golden brown and bubbly.
9. Remove from the air fryer and let cool for a few minutes before serving.

Nutritional Information (per serving, 1 stuffed mushroom)

-Calories: 150

-Fat: 11g

-Saturated Fat: 4g

-Cholesterol: 110mg

-Sodium: 280mg

-Carbohydrates: 5g

-Fiber: 2g

-Sugar: 2g-Protein: 8g

15. Chicken and Quinoa Bowls

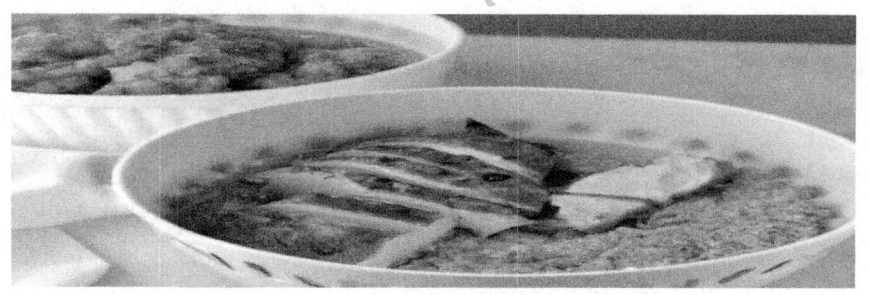

Ingredients

- 1 lb boneless, skinless chicken breast, diced
- Salt and pepper, to taste
- 1 cup uncooked quinoa
- 2 cups chicken broth
- 1 red bell pepper, diced
- 1 yellow bell pepper, diced
- 1 cup frozen corn
- 1/4 cup chopped fresh cilantro
- 1/4 cup diced red onion
- 2 cloves garlic, minced
- 1/4 cup fresh lime juice

Instructions

1 Rinse quinoa in a fine mesh strainer and drain.

2 Quinoa and chicken broth should be combined in a medium pot. Bring to a boil, reduce heat to low, cover and simmer for 18-20 minutes or until quinoa is tender and liquid is absorbed.

3 Allow the item to cool for a few minutes before taking it off the heat source.

4 400°F should be the air fryer's set temperature.

5 Season the chicken with salt and pepper and place in the air fryer. Cook for 10-12 minutes or until cooked through.

6 Remove the chicken from the air fryer and set it aside.

7 In the same air fryer add the bell peppers, corn, red onion, and garlic and cook for 8-10 minutes or until softened, stirring occasionally.

8 Stir in the lime juice, cilantro, and cooked chicken.

9 Serve the mixture over quinoa.

Nutritional Information (per serving, 1 cup of quinoa and 1 cup of the chicken mixture)

-Calories: 420

-Fat: 12g

-Saturated Fat: 2g

-Cholesterol: 65mg

-Sodium: 480mg

-Carbohydrates: 42g

-Fiber: 5g-Sugar: 4g-Protein: 35g

16. Chicken and Veggie Stir Fry

Ingredients

- 1 lb boneless, skinless chicken breast, cut into small strips
- 1 tbsp olive oil
- 1 tsp garlic powder
- 1 tsp onion powder
- Salt and pepper, to taste
- 1 red bell pepper, sliced
- 1 green bell pepper, sliced
- 1 yellow onion, sliced
- 2 cups broccoli florets
- 1 cup sliced mushrooms

Instructions

1 In a large bowl, combine the chicken strips, olive oil, garlic powder, onion powder, salt, and pepper. Toss to coat the chicken evenly.

2 Place the chicken in the air fryer basket and cook at 375°F for 10 minutes.

3 Add the red and green bell peppers, onion, broccoli, and mushrooms to the basket and cook for an additional 10 minutes or until the vegetables are tender and the chicken is cooked through.

4 Serve the stir fry over brown rice or quinoa, if desired.

Nutrition Information (per serving, assumes 4 servings):

- Calories: 233
- Total Fat: 9g
- Saturated Fat: 2g
- Cholesterol: 72mg
- Sodium: 97mg
- Total Carbohydrates: 12g
- Dietary Fiber: 3g
- Sugars: 5g
- Protein: 26g

17. Chili-Lime Tofu

Ingredients

- 1 block of firm tofu, pressed and cut into small cubes
- 1 tbsp olive oil
- 2 tbsp chili powder
- 1 tsp garlic powder
- 1 tsp onion powder
- Salt and pepper, to taste
- Juice of 1 lime

Instructions

1 In a large bowl, combine the tofu cubes, olive oil, chili powder, garlic powder, onion powder, salt, pepper, and lime juice. Toss to coat the tofu evenly.

2 Place the tofu in the air fryer basket and cook at 375°F for 20 minutes, shaking the basket every 5 minutes to ensure even cooking.

3 Serve the chili-lime tofu as a side dish or over a bed of brown rice or quinoa, if desired.

Nutrition Information (per serving, assumes 4 servings):

- Calories: 131
- Total Fat: 8g
- Saturated Fat: 1g
- Cholesterol: 0mg
- Sodium: 13mg
- Total Carbohydrates: 6g
- Dietary Fiber: 1g
- Sugars: 2g
- Protein: 10g

18. Crispy Baked Tofu

Ingredients

- 1 block of firm tofu, pressed and cut into small cubes
- 1 tbsp olive oil
- 1 tsp soy sauce
- 1 tsp nutritional yeast
- 1 tsp smoked paprika
- 1 tsp garlic powder
- Salt and pepper, to taste

Instructions

1 In a large bowl, combine the tofu cubes, olive oil, soy sauce, nutritional yeast, smoked paprika, garlic powder, salt, and pepper. Toss to coat the tofu evenly.

2 Place the tofu in the air fryer basket and cook at 375°F for 15 minutes.

3 Shake the basket every 5 minutes to ensure even cooking.

4 Cook for additional 5 minutes or until the tofu is crispy and golden brown.

5 Serve the crispy baked tofu as a side dish or add it to your favorite salad or sandwich.

Nutrition Information (per serving, assumes 4 servings):

- Calories: 98
- Total Fat: 7g
- Saturated Fat: 1g
- Cholesterol: 0mg
- Sodium: 174mg
- Total Carbohydrates: 3g
- Dietary Fiber: 1g
- Sugars: 1g
- Protein: 7g

19. Curried Vegetable Soup

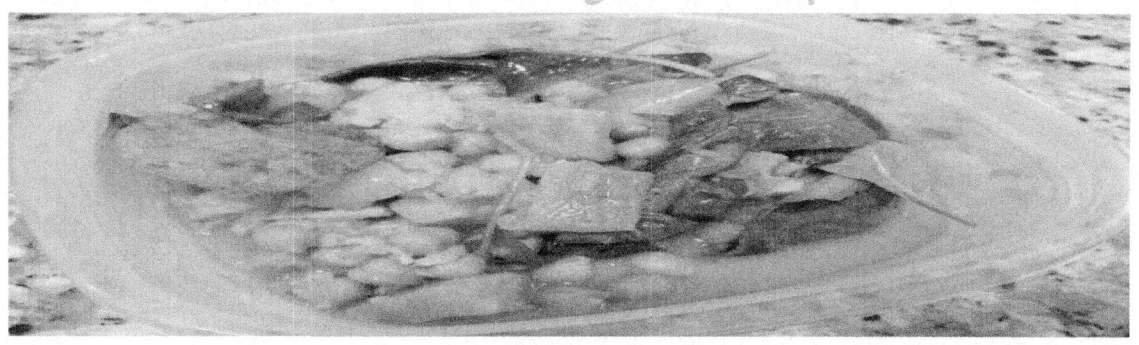

Ingredients

- 1 tbsp olive oil
- 1 onion, diced
- 2 cloves of garlic, minced
- 1 tbsp curry powder
- 2 cups of diced carrots
- 2 cups of diced potatoes
- 1 cup of diced celery
- 1 cup of diced bell pepper
- 4 cups of vegetable broth
- Salt and pepper, to taste

Instructions

1 In the air fryer basket, place the onion, garlic, and curry powder with 1 tbsp of olive oil, set the temperature to 375F, and cook for 5 minutes.

2 Add the vegetables (carrots, potatoes, celery, and bell pepper) and stir to combine.

3 Add the vegetable broth, salt, and pepper to the basket.

4 Cook for 20-25 minutes or until vegetables is tender.

5 Serve the curried vegetable soup with a sprinkle of chopped cilantro or parsley, if desired.

Nutrition Information (per serving, assumes 4 servings):

- Calories: 153
- Total Fat: 4g
- Saturated Fat: 1g
- Cholesterol: 0mg
- Sodium: 663mg
- Total Carbohydrates: 27g
- Dietary Fiber: 4g
- Sugars: 7g
- Protein: 3g

20. Egg and Cheese Rollups

Ingredients

- 4 large eggs

- 1/4 cup milk

- Salt and pepper, to taste

- 4 slices of deli turkey or ham

- 1/2 cup shredded cheese

- 1 tbsp butter or cooking spray (for greasing the air fryer basket)

Instructions

1 In a mixing bowl, whisk together the eggs, milk, salt, and pepper.

2 Grease the air fryer basket with butter or cooking spray.

3 Lay the turkey or ham slices on a cutting board or flat surface.

4 Divide the shredded cheese among the slices of turkey ham.

5 Roll up the slices tightly and secure them with toothpicks if needed.

6 Dip the roll-ups in the egg mixture, making sure they are fully coated.

7 Place the roll-ups in the air fryer basket and cook at 375°F for 10-12 minutes or until the eggs are cooked and the cheese is melted.

8 Serve the egg and cheese roll-ups warm, garnished with chopped chives or parsley if desired.

Nutrition Information (per serving, assumes 4 servings):

- Calories: 172

- Total Fat: 13g

- Saturated Fat: 6g

- Cholesterol: 220mg

- Sodium: 722mg

- Total Carbohydrates: 1g

- Dietary Fiber: 0g

- Sugars: 1g

- Protein: 14g

21. Falafel Wraps

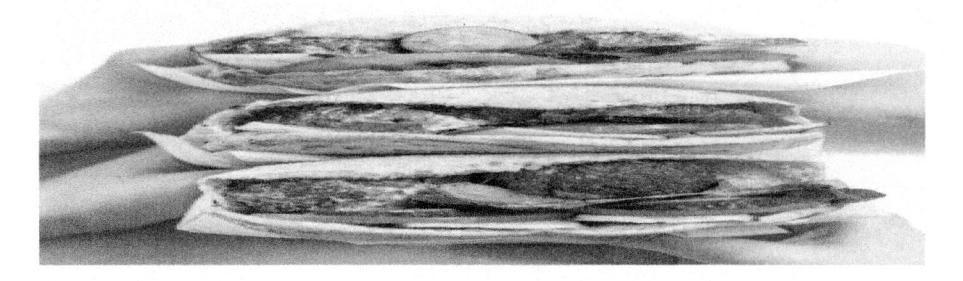

Ingredients

- 1 can of chickpeas, drained and rinsed
- 1/4 cup chopped onion
- 2 cloves of garlic, minced
- 2 tbsp parsley, chopped
- 2 tbsp cilantro, chopped
- 2 tbsp flour (can use gluten-free flour)
- 1 tsp ground cumin
- 1 tsp ground coriander
- Salt and pepper, to taste
- 2 tbsp olive oil
- Make four wraps using either whole wheat or gluten-free ingredients.
- Toppings of your choice (lettuce, tomato, cucumber, tzatziki sauce, hummus)

Instructions

1 In a food processor or blender, pulse the chickpeas, onion, garlic, parsley, cilantro, flour, cumin, coriander, salt, and pepper until a coarse mixture forms.

2 Shape the mixture into small balls or patties.

3 Brush the falafel balls or patties with olive oil.

4 Place the falafel in the air fryer basket and cook at 375°F for 15-20 minutes or until golden brown and crispy.

5 Serve the falafel in whole wheat or gluten-free wraps with toppings of your choice.

Nutrition Information (per serving, assumes 4 servings):

- Calories: 282
- Total Fat: 12g
- Saturated Fat: 2g
- Cholesterol: 0mg
- Sodium: 524mg
- Total Carbohydrates: 34g
- Dietary Fiber: 7g
- Sugars: 4g
- Protein: 10g

22. Greek Salad with Grilled Chicken

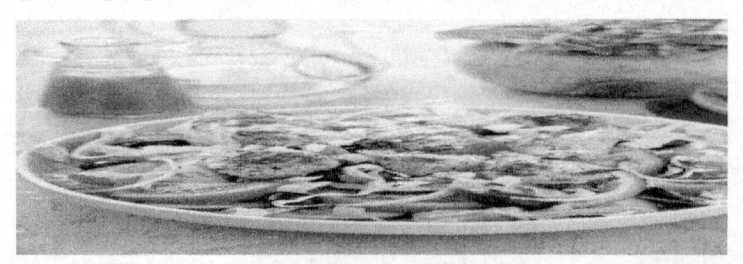

Ingredients

- 2 boneless, skinless chicken breasts
- 1 tsp olive oil
- 1 tsp dried oregano
- Salt and pepper, to taste
- 2 cups diced tomatoes
- 1 cup diced cucumber
- 1/2 cup sliced red onion
- 1/2 cup sliced Kalamata olives
- 1/4 cup crumbled feta cheese
- 1 tbsp red wine vinegar
- 1 tbsp olive oil
- 1 clove of garlic, minced
- Salt and pepper, to taste

Instructions

1 Season chicken breasts with 1 tsp of olive oil, dried oregano, salt, and pepper.

2 Place the chicken in the air fryer basket and cook at 375°F for 15-20 minutes or until cooked through.

3 In a large bowl, combine the tomatoes, cucumber, red onion, Kalamata olives, and feta cheese.

4 In a small bowl, whisk together the red wine vinegar, 1 tbsp of olive oil, garlic, salt, and pepper.

5 Add the vegetables to the dressing and toss until everything is evenly coated.

6 Slice the chicken breasts and add them to the salad.

7 Toss the salad again to combine.

8 Serve the Greek salad with grilled chicken warm or chilled.

Nutrition Information (per serving, assumes 4 servings):

- Calories: 231
- Total Fat: 17g
- Saturated Fat: 5g
- Cholesterol: 48mg
- Sodium: 531mg
- Total Carbohydrates: 8g
- Dietary Fiber: 2g
- Sugars: 4g
- Protein: 14g

23. Grilled Cheese and Tomato Sandwich

Ingredients

- Two slices of either whole wheat or gluten-free bread.
- 2 tbsp butter or margarine, at room temperature
- 2 slices of cheese (cheddar, American, or your favorite cheese)
- 2 slices of tomato
- Salt and pepper, to taste

Instructions

1 Spread either butter or margarine on one side of each slice of bread.

2 Place the cheese and tomato slices between the bread, and butter side out.

3 Season generously with salt and pepper, to taste.

4 Place the sandwich in the air fryer basket and cook at 375°F for 5-7 minutes or until the bread is golden brown and the cheese is melted.

5 Serve the grilled cheese and tomato sandwich warm, garnished with chopped chives or parsley if desired.

Nutrition Information (per serving, assumes 1 serving):

- Calories: 391
- Total Fat: 27g
- Saturated Fat: 16g
- Cholesterol: 70mg
- Sodium: 734mg
- Total Carbohydrates: 25g
- Dietary Fiber: 3g
- Sugars: 4g
- Protein: 12g

24. Kale and White Bean Soup

Ingredients

- 1 tbsp olive oil
- 1 onion, diced
- 2 cloves of garlic, minced
- 1 tsp dried thyme
- 1 tsp dried rosemary
- 1 tsp smoked paprika
- Salt and pepper, to taste
- 4 cups of vegetable broth
- 1 can of white beans, drained and rinsed
- 2 cups of chopped kale
- 1/4 cup grated Parmesan cheese (optional)

Instructions

1 In the air fryer basket, place the onion, garlic, thyme, rosemary, smoked paprika, and olive oil. Set the temperature to 375F and cook for 5 minutes.

2 Add the vegetable broth, white beans, kale, salt, and pepper to the basket.

3 Cook for 20-25 minutes or until the kale is wilted and the vegetables are tender.

4 If desired, the soup can be served with grated Parmesan cheese.

Nutrition Information (per serving, assumes 4 servings):

- Calories: 156
- Total Fat: 5g
- Saturated Fat: 1g
- Cholesterol: 3mg
- Sodium: 835mg
- Total Carbohydrates: 20g
- Dietary Fiber: 5g
- Sugars: 2g
- Protein: 7g

25. Lentil and Vegetable Stew

Ingredients

- 1 tbsp olive oil
- 1 onion, diced
- 2 cloves of garlic, minced
- 1 cup diced carrots
- 1 cup diced potatoes
- 1 cup diced celery
- 1 cup diced bell pepper
- 1 cup green or brown lentils, rinsed and drained
- 4 cups of vegetable broth
- 1 tsp dried thyme
- 1 tsp dried rosemary
- Salt and pepper, to taste

Instructions

1 In the air fryer basket, place the onion, garlic, thyme, rosemary, and olive oil. Set the temperature to 375F and cook for 5 minutes.

2 Add the vegetables (carrots, potatoes, celery, bell pepper, lentils), vegetable broth, salt, and pepper to the basket.

3 Cook for 20-25 minutes or until the lentils and vegetables are tender.

4 Serve the lentil and vegetable stew with a sprinkle of chopped cilantro or parsley, if desired.

Nutrition Information (per serving, assumes 4 servings):

- Calories: 259
- Total Fat: 4g
- Saturated Fat: 1g
- Cholesterol: 0mg
- Sodium: 703mg
- Total Carbohydrates: 43g
- Dietary Fiber: 13g
- Sugars: 6g
- Protein: 14g

26. Loaded Sweet Potato Skins

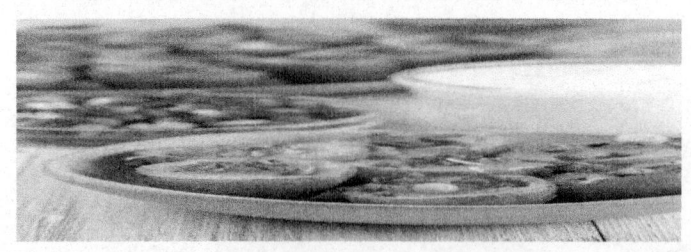

Ingredients

- 4 medium sweet potatoes, scrubbed and dried

- 1 tbsp olive oil

- Salt and pepper, to taste

- 1/2 cup shredded cheddar cheese

- 1/4 cup diced bacon

- 1/4 cup diced green onions

- 2 tbsp sour cream (optional)

Instructions

1 Preheat the air fryer to 375°F.

2 Cut the sweet potatoes in half lengthwise and scoop out the flesh, leaving about 1/4 inch of potato flesh inside the skin.

3 Brush the sweet potato skins with olive oil and season with salt and pepper.

4 Place the sweet potato skins in the air fryer basket and cook for 15-20 minutes or until the skins are crispy and tender.

5 Remove the sweet potatoes from the air fryer and top them with shredded cheese, diced bacon, and green onions.

6 Return the sweet potatoes to the air fryer and cook for an additional 5-7 minutes or until the cheese is melted.

7 Serve the loaded sweet potato skins with a dollop of sour cream, if desired.

Nutrition Information (per serving, assumes 4 servings):

- Calories: 220

- Total Fat: 12g

- Saturated Fat: 5g

- Cholesterol: 23mg

- Sodium: 358mg

- Total Carbohydrates: 21g

- Dietary Fiber: 2g

- Sugars: 5g

- Protein: 7g

27. Roasted Chickpeas

Ingredients

- 1 can of chickpeas, drained and rinsed
- 1 tbsp olive oil
- 1 tsp ground cumin
- 1 tsp smoked paprika
- 1/2 tsp garlic powder
- Salt and pepper, to taste

Instructions

1 Preheat the air fryer to 375°F.

2 In a mixing bowl, combine the chickpeas with olive oil, cumin, smoked paprika, garlic powder, salt, and pepper, and toss until evenly coated.

3 Place the chickpeas in the air fryer basket and cook for 15-20 minutes or until crispy.

4 Every five minutes, give the basket a vigorous shake to ensure that the food is cooking evenly.

5 Serve the roasted chickpeas warm or at room temperature as a snack or add-on to your salad or grain bowl.

Nutrition Information (per serving, assumes 4 servings):

- Calories: 150
- Total Fat: 6g
- Saturated Fat: 1g
- Cholesterol: 0mg
- Sodium: 266mg
- Total Carbohydrates: 19g
- Dietary Fiber: 4g
- Sugars: 2g
- Protein: 5g

28. Roasted Veggie and Quinoa Salad

Ingredients

- 1 cup of quinoa

- 2 cups of mixed vegetables (carrots, bell peppers, onions, zucchini, etc.)

- 1 tbsp olive oil

- 1 tsp dried oregano

- 2 tbsp chopped parsley or cilantro

- Salt and pepper, to taste

- 1/4 cup crumbled feta cheese

- 2 tbsp lemon juice

Instructions

1 Cook the quinoa according to package instructions, and set aside.

2 Set the air fryer to 375°F.

3 In a bowl, combine the mixed vegetables with olive oil, oregano, salt, and pepper and toss them together.

4 Place the vegetables in the air fryer basket and cook for 15-20 minutes or until tender and golden brown.

5 In a large bowl, combine the cooked quinoa, roasted vegetables, feta cheese, lemon juice, and parsley or cilantro.

6 Toss the salad well to combine.

7 Serve the roasted veggie and quinoa salad warm or chilled.

Nutrition Information (per serving, assumes 4 servings):

- Calories: 280

- Total Fat: 11g

- Saturated Fat: 3g

- Cholesterol: 10mg

- Sodium: 191mg

- Total Carbohydrates: 34g

- Dietary Fiber: 5g

- Sugars: 4g

- Protein: 11g

29. Skinny French Toast Sticks

Ingredients

- 4 slices of whole wheat or gluten-free bread, cut into sticks
- 1 large egg
- 1/4 cup almond milk
- 1 tsp vanilla extract
- 1 tsp ground cinnamon
- 1 tsp powdered sugar (optional)
- 1 tsp of olive oil
- Salt and pepper, to taste

Instructions

1 Preheat the air fryer to 375°F.

2 In a shallow dish, whisk together the egg, almond milk, vanilla extract, cinnamon, salt, and pepper.

3 Dip the breadsticks in the egg mixture, making sure they are well coated.

4 Place the breadsticks in the air fryer basket and brush them with olive oil.

5 Cook for 10-12 minutes until the outside is golden brown and crunchy.

6 erve the French toast sticks with powdered sugar, syrup, or your favorite topping.

Nutrition Information (per serving, assumes 4 servings):

- Calories: 153
- Total Fat: 5g
- Saturated Fat: 1g
- Cholesterol: 54mg
- Sodium: 190mg
- Total Carbohydrates: 20g
- Dietary Fiber: 2g
- Sugars: 4g
- Protein: 6g

30. Vegetable and Bean Burritos

Ingredients

- 4 whole wheat or gluten-free burrito-size tortillas
- 1 can of black beans, drained and rinsed
- 1 cup diced bell peppers
- 1 cup diced onion
- 1 cup diced zucchini
- 1 cup diced mushrooms
- 1 tbsp olive oil
- 1 tsp chili powder
- 1 tsp cumin
- Salt and pepper, to taste
- 1 cup shredded cheddar cheese
- 1/4 cup diced green onions
- 1/4 cup diced fresh cilantro
- 1/4 cup sour cream (optional)

Instructions

1 Preheat the air fryer to 375°F.

2 Combine the olive oil, chili powder, cumin, salt, and pepper in a mixing bowl. Toss in the veggies to coat.

3 In another mixing bowl, mash the black beans with a fork or potato masher.

4 Lay out the tortillas, and divide the mashed black beans and the vegetable mixture among them.

5 Sprinkle shredded cheddar cheese, green onions, and cilantro on top of the vegetables and beans.

6 Roll up the tortillas, tucking in the sides as you go, to form burritos.

7 Place the burritos in the air fryer basket, seam side down.

8 Cook for 10-12 minutes or until golden brown and crispy.

9 Serve the burritos with sour cream or your favorite toppings.

Nutrition Information (per serving, assumes 4 servings):

- Calories: 356
- Total Fat: 14g
- Saturated Fat: 6g
- Cholesterol: 24mg
- Sodium: 515mg

- Total Carbohydrates: 42g   - Dietary Fiber: 10g   - Sugars: 3g   - Protein: 16g

PART FOUR

Dinner

1. Air Fryer Sesame Chicken

Ingredients

- 1 pound boneless, skinless chicken breasts, cut into bite-sized pieces
- 1/4 cup cornstarch
- 1/4 teaspoon salt
- 1/4 teaspoon black pepper
- 1/4 cup low-sodium soy sauce
- 2 tablespoons rice vinegar
- 1 tablespoon sesame oil
- 1 tablespoon brown sugar substitute (such as Stevia or Erythritol)
- 1 teaspoon minced garlic
- 1/4 teaspoon red pepper flakes (optional)
- 2 tablespoons sesame seeds

Instructions

1 In a small bowl, mix together the cornstarch, pepper, and salt. Toss in the chicken pieces to coat.

2 Combine soy sauce, sesame oil, rice vinegar, brown sugar substitute, garlic, and red pepper flakes in a small bowl. Mix it together until all ingredients are well mixed.

3 Place chicken in the air fryer basket and spray with cooking spray. Cook at 400°F for 12-15 minutes, or until cooked through and golden brown.

4 In a small saucepan, heat sesame seeds over medium heat until they become a golden brown color.

5 Remove the chicken from the air fryer and toss it with the soy sauce mixture.

6 Sprinkle with toasted sesame seeds and serve.

Nutritional Information (per serving, assuming 4 servings):

- Calories: 161
- Protein: 24g
- Carbohydrates: 7g
- Fat: 4g
- Saturated Fat: 1g
- Cholesterol: 66mg
- Sodium: 722mg
- Fiber: 1g   - Sugar: 2g

2. Air Fryer Cauliflower Wings

Ingredients

- 1 head of cauliflower, cut into small florets
- 1/2 cup almond flour
- 1/4 cup grated parmesan cheese
- 1 teaspoon garlic powder
- 1/2 teaspoon onion powder
- 1/4 teaspoon salt
- 1/4 teaspoon black pepper
- 1/2 cup unsweetened almond milk
- 2 tablespoons hot sauce
- 1 teaspoon olive oil

Instructions

1 In a shallow dish, combine almond flour, parmesan cheese, garlic powder, onion powder, salt, and pepper.

2 In a different bowl, combine almond milk, hot sauce, and olive oil by whisking them together.

3 Dip cauliflower florets into the milk mixture, then coat in the almond flour mixture.

4 Place cauliflower in the air fryer basket and spray with cooking spray. Air-fry at 400 degrees F for 12-15 minutes or until golden brown and crispy.

5 You may serve this dish with any type of dipping sauce you desire.

Nutritional Information (per serving, assuming 4 servings):

- Calories: 128
- Protein: 6g
- Carbohydrates: 8g
- Fat: 9g
- Saturated Fat: 2g
- Cholesterol: 3mg
- Sodium: 511mg
- Fiber: 2g
- Sugar: 3g

3. Air Fryer Lemon Garlic Shrimp

Ingredients

- 1 pound large shrimp, peeled and deveined

- 2 cloves of garlic, minced

- 1/4 cup lemon juice

- 2 tablespoons olive oil

- 1/4 teaspoon salt

- 1/4 teaspoon black pepper

- 1 tablespoon fresh parsley, chopped (for garnish)

Instructions

1 In a large bowl, combine garlic, lemon juice, olive oil, salt, and pepper. Add shrimp and toss to coat.

2 Place shrimp in the air fryer basket and spray with cooking spray. Air-fry the shrimp for 8-10 minutes at 400 degrees F, or until pink and cooked through.

3 Finish off the dish by garnishing with fresh parsley and then serve.

Nutritional Information (per serving, assuming 4 servings):

- Calories: 192

- Protein: 24g

- Carbohydrates: 2g

- Fat: 11g

- Saturated Fat: 2g

- Cholesterol: 215mg

- Sodium: 300mg

- Fiber: 0g

- Sugar: 0g

4. Air Fryer Meatball Subs

Ingredients

- 1/4 cup grated parmesan cheese
- 1/4 cup almond flour
- 1/4 cup finely chopped onion
- 1 pound ground turkey or beef
- 2 cloves of garlic, minced
- 1/4 teaspoon salt
- 1/4 teaspoon black pepper
- 1 egg
- 2 cups shredded mozzarella cheese
- 1/4 cup marinara sauce
- 4 whole wheat sub rolls

Instructions

1 In a large bowl, combine ground meat, parmesan cheese, almond flour, onion, garlic, salt, pepper, and egg. Mix well to combine.

2 Create the meatballs of your choosing using the mixture.

3 Place meatballs in the air fryer basket and spray with cooking spray. Bake in an air fryer set to 400 degrees Fahrenheit for 12-15 minutes, or until the food is cooked through and has a golden-brown color.

4 While the meatballs are cooking, slice the sub rolls in half lengthwise. Coat the interior of each roll with marinara sauce.

5 Once the meatballs are cooked, place them on the bottom half of the rolls.

6 Top each meatball sub with shredded mozzarella cheese.

7 Place the subs back in the air fryer for an additional 2-3 minutes or until the cheese is melted.

8 Serve warm.

Nutritional Information (per serving, assuming 4 servings):

- Calories: 596
- Protein: 45g
- Carbohydrates: 37g
- Fat: 30g
- Saturated Fat: 12g
- Cholesterol: 143mg
- Sodium: 784mg
- Fiber: 4g   - Sugar: 4g

5. Air Fryer Parmesan Crusted Pork Chops

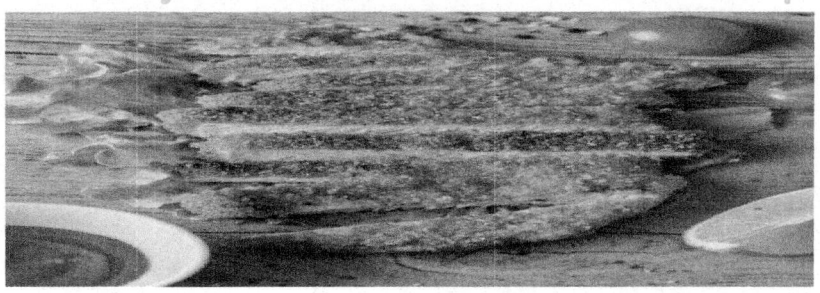

Ingredients

- 4 boneless pork chops (about 1/2-inch thick)
- 1/4 cup grated parmesan cheese
- 1/4 cup almond flour
- 1/4 teaspoon salt
- 1/4 teaspoon black pepper
- 1 egg
- 1 tablespoon olive oil

Instructions

1 In a shallow dish, combine parmesan cheese, almond flour, salt, and pepper.

2 In a different bowl, whisk the egg.

3 Dip pork chops in the beaten egg, then coat in the parmesan mixture.

4 Coat the pork chops with olive oil using a brush.

5 Place pork chops in the air fryer basket and spray with cooking spray. Air-fry at 400 degrees F for 12-15 minutes or until cooked through and golden brown.

Nutritional Information (per serving, assuming 4 servings):

- Calories: 273
- Protein: 31g
- Carbohydrates: 3g
- Fat: 17g
- Saturated Fat: 5g
- Cholesterol: 119mg
- Sodium: 376mg
- Fiber: 1g
- Sugar: 0g

6. Air Fryer Stuffed Bell Peppers

Ingredients

- 4 large bell peppers, any color
- 1 pound ground turkey
- 1/2 cup diced onions
- 1/2 cup diced tomatoes
- 1/4 cup diced mushrooms
- 2 cloves of garlic, minced
- 1/4 cup cooked quinoa
- 1/4 cup grated parmesan cheese
- 1/4 teaspoon salt
- 1/4 teaspoon black pepper

Instructions

1 Cut off the tops of the bell peppers and remove the seeds and membranes.

2 In a large skillet, cook ground turkey until browned. Drain off any excess fat.

3 Add diced onions, tomatoes, mushrooms, and garlic. Cook for a few minutes until vegetables are softened.

4 Stir in cooked quinoa, parmesan cheese, salt, and pepper.

5 Stuff the bell peppers with the turkey mixture and place them in the air fryer basket.

6 Air-fry at 400 degrees F for 20-25 minutes or until the peppers are tender and the filling is hot and bubbly.

Nutritional Information (per serving, assuming 4 servings):

- Calories: 243
- Protein: 22g
- Carbohydrates: 16g
- Fat: 10g
- Saturated Fat: 3g
- Cholesterol: 65mg
- Sodium: 259mg
- Fiber: 4g
- Sugar: 7g

7. Air Fryer Teriyaki Tofu

Ingredients

- 1 pound firm tofu, drained and pressed
- 1/4 cup low-sodium soy sauce
- 2 tablespoons rice vinegar
- 1 tablespoon brown sugar substitute (such as Stevia or Erythritol)
- 1 teaspoon minced garlic
- 1 teaspoon grated ginger
- 1 tablespoon cornstarch
- 1 tablespoon water
- Sesame seeds and green onions for garnish (optional)

Instructions

1 In a small bowl, whisk together soy sauce, rice vinegar, brown sugar substitute, garlic, and ginger.

2 Slice the tofu into pieces that are 1/2 inch thick.

3 In a small bowl, whisk together cornstarch and water to make a slurry.

4 Dip each tofu slice in the teriyaki sauce and then coat in the cornstarch slurry.

5 Place tofu in the air fryer basket and spray it with cooking spray. Air-fry at 400 degrees F for 12-15 minutes or until crispy and golden brown.

6 If you want, apply more teriyaki sauce while brushing.

7 Garnish with sesame seeds and green onions (if using) and serve.

Nutritional Information (per serving, assuming 4 servings):

- Calories: 149
- Protein: 14g
- Carbohydrates: 10g
- Fat: 7g
- Saturated Fat: 1g
- Cholesterol: 0mg
- Sodium: 789mg
- Fiber: 1g
- Sugar: 3g

8. Air Fryer Zucchini Fries

Ingredients

- 2 medium zucchinis, cut into wedges
- 1/4 cup almond flour
- 1/4 cup grated parmesan cheese
- 1/4 teaspoon salt
- 1/4 teaspoon black pepper
- 1 egg
- Cooking spray

Instructions

1 Combine almond flour, parmesan cheese, salt, and pepper in a shallow dish.

2 Beat the egg in another bowl.

3 Dip zucchini wedges in the beaten egg, then coat in the almond flour mixture.

4 Place zucchini wedges in the air fryer basket and spray with cooking spray.

5 Air-fry at 400 degrees F for 8-10 minutes or until golden brown and crispy.

Nutritional Information (per serving, assuming 4 servings):

- Calories: 105
- Protein: 5g
- Carbohydrates: 8g
- Fat: 6g
- Saturated Fat: 2g
- Cholesterol: 62mg
- Sodium: 337mg
- Fiber: 2g
- Sugar: 3g

9. Black Bean and Sweet Potato Tacos

Ingredients

- 1 can of black beans, drained and rinsed
- 1/2 cup diced onions
- 1/2 cup diced tomatoes
- 1/4 cup diced bell pepper
- 2 cloves of garlic, minced
- 2 medium sweet potatoes, peeled and diced
- 1 teaspoon chili powder
- 1/2 teaspoon cumin
- 1/4 teaspoon salt
- Fresh cilantro for garnish (optional)
- 1/4 teaspoon black pepper
- 1/4 cup shredded cheddar cheese
- 8 corn tortillas

Instructions

1 In a large bowl, combine sweet potatoes, black beans, onions, tomatoes, bell pepper, garlic, chili powder, cumin, salt, and pepper.

2 Place the sweet potato mixture in the air fryer basket and spray it with cooking spray. Air-fry at 400 degrees F for 20-25 minutes or until the sweet potatoes are tender and lightly browned.

3 While the sweet potato mixture is cooking, heat the tortillas in the oven or on a stovetop griddle until warm.

4 To assemble the tacos, spoon some of the sweet potato mixtures onto a tortilla and sprinkle it with shredded cheese.

5 Garnish with fresh cilantro (if using) and serve.

Nutritional Information (per serving, assuming 8 servings):

- Calories: 214
- Protein: 8g
- Carbohydrates: 40g
- Fat: 4g
- Saturated Fat: 2g
- Cholesterol: 7mg
- Sodium: 245mg
- Fiber: 5g
- Sugar: 7g

10. Air Fryer BBQ Pork Tenderloin

Ingredients

- 1 pound pork tenderloin
- 1/4 cup BBQ sauce
- 1 tablespoon olive oil
- 1 teaspoon smoked paprika
- 1/4 teaspoon garlic powder
- 1/4 teaspoon onion powder
- 1/4 teaspoon salt
- 1/4 teaspoon black pepper

Instructions

1 In a small bowl, mix together BBQ sauce, olive oil, smoked paprika, garlic powder, onion powder, salt, and pepper.

2 Rub the pork tenderloin with the BBQ sauce mixture.

3 Place the pork tenderloin in the air fryer basket and spray it with cooking spray. Air-fry at 400 degrees F for 20-25 minutes or until the internal temperature reaches 145°F.

4 Let it rest for 5 minutes before slicing and serving.

Nutritional Information (per serving, assuming 4 servings):

- Calories: 175
- Protein: 25g
- Carbohydrates: 7g
- Fat: 6g
- Saturated Fat: 1g
- Cholesterol: 74mg
- Sodium: 474mg
- Fiber: 0g
- Sugar: 6g

11. Air Fryer Crispy Tofu Nuggets

Ingredients

- Cooking spray
- 1 block of firm tofu, drained and pressed
- 1/4 cup unsweetened almond milk
- 1/4 cup cornstarch
- 1/4 cup panko breadcrumbs
- 1/4 teaspoon salt
- 1/4 cup grated parmesan cheese
- 1/4 teaspoon black pepper

Instructions

1 Cut the tofu into bite-size nuggets.

2 Mix the cornstarch, salt, and pepper together in a shallow dish.

3 In a separate bowl, mix together the almond milk, panko breadcrumbs, and parmesan cheese.

4 Dip the tofu nuggets in the cornstarch mixture, then in the almond milk mixture, then again in the cornstarch mixture.

5 Place the tofu nuggets in the air fryer basket and spray them with cooking spray.

6 Air fried for 12 to 15 minutes at 400 degrees F, or crispy and until golden.

Nutritional Information (per serving, assuming 4 servings):

- Calories: 136
- Protein: 11g
- Carbohydrates: 12g
- Fat: 6g
- Saturated Fat: 2g
- Cholesterol: 5mg
- Sodium: 467mg
- Fiber: 2g
- Sugar: 2g

12. Air Fryer Harissa Chicken Skewers

Ingredients

- 1 pound boneless, skinless chicken breasts, cut into 1-inch cubes
- 1/4 cup harissa paste
- 2 cloves of garlic, minced
- 2 tablespoons olive oil
- 1/4 teaspoon salt
- 1/4 teaspoon black pepper
- Lemon wedges for serving (optional)

Instructions

1 In a large bowl, mix together harissa paste, garlic, olive oil, salt, and pepper.

2 Add chicken cubes to the bowl and toss to coat.

3 Thread chicken cubes onto skewers by first placing one cube of chicken onto the end of the skewer. Then, add another cube of chicken, followed by a third cube of chicken until the skewer is almost full. Secure the last cube with a twist of the skewer and repeat the process until all cubes of chicken have been threaded onto the skewers.

4 Place the skewers in the air fryer basket and spray them with cooking spray. Air-fry at 400 degrees F for 12-15 minutes or until the chicken is cooked through and golden brown.

5 Serve with lemon wedges (optional).

Nutritional Information (per serving, assuming 4 servings):

- Calories: 234
- Protein: 27g
- Carbohydrates: 3g
- Fat: 13g
- Saturated Fat: 2g
- Cholesterol: 73mg
- Sodium: 516mg
- Fiber: 1g
- Sugar: 1g

13. Air Fryer Mushroom and Onion Quiche

Ingredients

- 1 pre-made pie crust
- 1/2 cup diced onions
- 1/2 cup diced mushrooms
- 4 eggs
- 1/2 cup heavy cream
- 1/4 cup grated parmesan cheese
- 1/4 teaspoon salt
- 1/4 teaspoon black pepper

Instructions

1 Preheat the air fryer to 350F.

2 In a skillet, cook onions and mushrooms until softened.

3 In a large bowl, whisk together eggs, cream, parmesan cheese, salt, and pepper.

4 Stir in cooked onions and mushrooms.

5 Empty the mixture into the pie crust and even out the surface.

6 Place the quiche in the air fryer basket and air fry for 15-20 minutes or until the center is set and the crust is golden brown.

7 Allow it to cool for 5 minutes before slicing and serving.

Nutritional Information (per serving, assuming 8 servings):

- Calories: 218
- Protein: 7g
- Carbohydrates: 15g
- Fat: 15g
- Saturated Fat: 7g
- Cholesterol: 158mg
- Sodium: 325mg
- Fiber: 1g
- Sugar: 2g

14. Air Fryer Pesto Chicken

Ingredients

- 4 boneless, skinless chicken breasts
- 1/4 cup prepared pesto
- 1/4 cup grated parmesan cheese
- 1/4 teaspoon salt
- Lemon wedges for serving (optional)
- 1/4 teaspoon black pepper

Instructions

1 In a small bowl, mix together pesto, parmesan cheese, salt, and pepper.

2 Place chicken breasts in a shallow dish and brush with the pesto mixture.

3 Place chicken in the air fryer basket and spray with cooking spray. Air-fry at 400 degrees F for 12-15 minutes or until the internal temperature reaches 165°F.

4 Serve with lemon wedges (if desired).

Nutritional Information (per serving, assuming 4 servings):

- Calories: 260
- Protein: 39g
- Carbohydrates: 2g
- Fat: 12g
- Saturated Fat: 3g
- Cholesterol: 108mg
- Sodium: 437mg
- Fiber: 1g
- Sugar: 1g

15. Air Fryer Rosemary Roasted Potatoes

Ingredients

- 2 pounds of baby potatoes, halved
- 2 tablespoons olive oil
- 2 teaspoons dried rosemary
- 1/4 teaspoon salt
- 1/4 teaspoon black pepper

Instructions

1 In a large bowl, toss potatoes with olive oil, rosemary, salt, and pepper.

2 Put the potatoes in the air fryer basket, then spray them with cooking spray.

3 Air-fry at 400 degrees F for 20-25 minutes or until golden brown and crispy.

Nutritional Information (per serving, assuming 4 servings):

- Calories: 216
- Protein: 3g
- Carbohydrates: 40g
- Fat: 6g
- Saturated Fat: 1g
- Cholesterol: 0mg
- Sodium: 260mg
- Fiber: 3g
- Sugar: 2g

16. Air Fryer Spicy Tuna Rolls

Ingredients

- 2 cans of tuna in water, drained
- 2 tablespoons mayonnaise
- 2 tablespoons sriracha sauce
- 2 teaspoons sesame oil
- 1/4 teaspoon salt
- 1/4 teaspoon black pepper
- 1 avocado, thinly sliced (optional)
- 8 sheets of sushi nori
- 4 cups cooked sushi rice

Instructions

1 In a medium bowl, mix together tuna, mayonnaise, sriracha sauce, sesame oil, salt, and pepper.

2 Place a sheet of sushi nori on a bamboo sushi rolling mat or a clean kitchen towel.

3 Spread 1/2 cup of sushi rice over the nori sheet, leaving a 1/2-inch border at the top.

4 Place 2 tablespoons of the tuna mixture on the rice.

5 Add a few slices of avocado (if using) on top of the tuna mixture.

6 Roll the sushi mat tightly to form a tight cylinder.

7 Repeat using the remaining ingredients.

8 Place the sushi rolls in the air fryer basket and spray them with cooking spray.

9 Air-fry at 400 degrees F for 8-10 minutes or until golden brown and crispy.

Nutritional Information (per serving, assuming 8 servings):

- Calories: 298
- Protein: 18g
- Carbohydrates: 42g
- Fat: 8g
- Saturated Fat: 1g
- Cholesterol: 25mg
- Sodium: 632mg
- Fiber: 2g
- Sugar: 1g

17. Air Fryer Spinach and Feta Stuffed Chicken Breasts

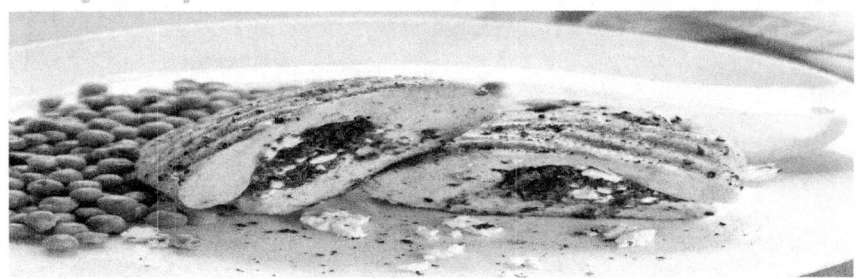

Ingredients

- 4 boneless, skinless chicken breasts
- 1 cup chopped fresh spinach
- 1/4 cup crumbled feta cheese
- 2 cloves of garlic, minced
- 1/4 teaspoon salt
- 1/4 teaspoon black pepper
- 1 tablespoon olive oil

Instructions

1 In a small bowl, mix together spinach, feta cheese, garlic, salt, and pepper.

2 Make a pocket in the side of each chicken breast, but don't cut all the way through.

3 Stuff each chicken breast with a spinach mixture.

4 Coat the chicken with olive oil using a brush.

5 Place the chicken breasts in the air fryer basket and spray them with cooking spray.

6 Air-fry at 400 degrees F for 20-25 minutes or until the internal temperature reaches 165°F.

Nutritional Information (per serving, assuming 4 servings):

- Calories: 217
- Protein: 33g
- Carbohydrates: 1g
- Fat: 9g
- Saturated Fat: 3g
- Cholesterol: 108mg
- Sodium: 394mg
- Fiber: 0g
- Sugar: 0g

18. Air Fryer Turkey Meatballs

Ingredients

- 1 pound ground turkey
- 1/4 cup diced onions
- 1/4 cup diced red bell pepper
- 2 cloves of garlic, minced
- 1 egg
- 2 tablespoons breadcrumbs
- 1 teaspoon dried oregano
- 1/4 teaspoon salt
- 1/4 teaspoon black pepper
- Cooking spray

Instructions

1 Combine ground turkey, onions, red bell pepper, garlic, egg, breadcrumbs, oregano, salt, and pepper in a large mixing bowl.

2 Roll the mixture into a 1 1/2-inch meatball.

3 Place meatballs in the air fryer basket and spray with cooking spray.

4 Air-fry at 400 degrees F for 12-15 minutes or until the internal temperature reaches 165°F.

Nutritional Information (per serving, assuming 4 servings):

- Calories: 255
- Protein: 32g
- Carbohydrates: 4g
- Fat: 13g
- Saturated Fat: 4g
- Cholesterol: 169mg
- Sodium: 437mg
- Fiber: 1g
- Sugar: 2g

19. Air Fryer Vegetable and Tofu Korma

Ingredients

- 1 cup diced vegetables (such as bell peppers, onions, carrots, and potatoes)
- 1 cup canned diced tomatoes
- 1 block of firm tofu, drained and pressed
- 1/4 cup coconut milk
- 2 cloves of garlic, minced
- 2 tablespoons korma curry paste
- 1 tablespoon olive oil
- 1/4 teaspoon salt
- 1/4 teaspoon black pepper
- Fresh cilantro for garnish (optional)

Instructions

1 Cut the tofu into small cubes.

2 In a large bowl, mix together the vegetables, canned tomatoes, coconut milk, garlic, curry paste, olive oil, salt, and pepper.

3 Toss the tofu chunks into the mixture to coat.

4 Place the mixture in the air fryer basket and spray it with cooking spray.

5 Air-fry at 400 degrees F for 20-25 minutes or until the vegetables are tender and the tofu is golden brown.

6 Garnish with fresh cilantro (if desired) and serve over rice or with naan bread.

Nutritional Information (per serving, assuming 4 servings):

- Calories: 218
- Protein: 11g
- Carbohydrates: 22g
- Fat: 12g
- Saturated Fat: 6g
- Cholesterol: 0mg
- Sodium: 517mg

20. Edamame and Avocado Salad

Ingredients

- 1 cup edamame, shelled and thawed
- 1 avocado, diced
- 1 tablespoon olive oil
- 1 teaspoon cumin
- Salt and pepper to taste
- 1 tablespoon lime juice
- 1 tablespoon chopped cilantro

Instructions

1 Preheat your air fryer to 400°F.

2 In a small bowl, mix together the olive oil, cumin, salt, and pepper.

3 Place the edamame in the air fryer basket and drizzle the oil mixture over it. Toss to coat.

4 Air fry for 8-10 minutes, or until crispy and golden brown.

5 In a large bowl, combine the air-fried edamame, diced avocado, lime juice, and cilantro. Toss to combine.

6 Serve immediately and enjoy.

Nutritional Information (per serving):

- Calories: 200
- Total Fat: 16g
- Saturated Fat: 2g
- Cholesterol: 0mg
- Sodium: 10mg
- Total Carbohydrates: 13g
- Dietary Fiber: 7g
- Sugars: 1g
- Protein: 7g

21. Skinny Cauliflower Mac and Cheese

Ingredients

- 1 head cauliflower, cut into small florets
- 1/4 cup of low-fat milk
- 1/4 cup grated Parmesan cheese
- 1/4 cup grated cheddar cheese
- 1 tablespoon flour
- Salt and pepper to taste
- 1 tablespoon olive oil
- 1 teaspoon dried basil

Instructions

1 Preheat your air fryer to 400°F.

2 Warm the milk in a saucepan over medium heat. Whisk in the flour until combined and cook for 1-2 minutes, or until the mixture thickens.

3 Remove the pan from heat and stir in the Parmesan cheese, cheddar cheese, salt, and pepper.

4 In a large bowl, toss the cauliflower florets with olive oil and dried basil.

5 Place the cauliflower in the air fryer basket and air fry for 12-15 minutes, or until tender and lightly browned.

6 Remove the cauliflower from the air fryer and toss it with the cheese sauce.

7 Return the cauliflower to the air fryer and cook for an additional 2-3 minutes, or until the cheese is melted and bubbly.

8 Serve immediately and enjoy.

Nutritional Information (per serving):

- Calories: 156
- Total Fat: 9g
- Saturated Fat: 4g
- Cholesterol: 17mg
- Sodium: 179mg
- Total Carbohydrates: 12g
- Dietary Fiber: 5g
- Sugars: 4g
- Protein: 10g

22. Vegetable and Quinoa Shepherd's Pie

Ingredients

- 1 cup mixed vegetables (such as carrots, peas, and corn)
- 1/2 cup vegetable broth
- 1/4 cup of low-fat milk
- 1 tablespoon flour
- 1 tablespoon olive oil
- 1 cup cooked quinoa
- 1 teaspoon dried thyme
- 1/2 cup grated cheddar cheese
- Salt and pepper to taste

Instructions

1 Preheat your air fryer to 400°F.

2 In a small saucepan, heat the vegetable broth over medium heat. Whisk in the flour until combined and cook for 1-2 minutes, or until the mixture thickens.

3 Remove the pan from heat and stir in the low-fat milk, thyme, salt, and pepper.

4 In a large bowl, toss the mixed vegetables with olive oil, salt, and pepper.

5 In a baking dish, layer the cooked quinoa, and mixed vegetables and pour the sauce over the top. Cover the top with grated cheese.

6 Place the baking dish in the air fryer and air fry for 12-15 minutes, or until the cheese is melted and bubbly.

7 Serve immediately and enjoy.

Nutritional Information (per serving):

- Calories: 312
- Total Fat: 14g
- Saturated Fat: 5g
- Cholesterol: 21mg
- Sodium: 449mg
- Total Carbohydrates: 34g
- Dietary Fiber: 6g
- Sugars: 7g
- Protein: 15g

23. Orange and Almond Tofu Stir-fry

Ingredients

- 1 block of firm tofu, drained and cut into cubes
- 1 orange, juiced and zested
- 1 tablespoon soy sauce
- 1 tablespoon rice vinegar
- 1 tablespoon cornstarch
- 1 tablespoon olive oil
- 1 teaspoon grated ginger
- 1/2 cup slivered almonds
- Salt and pepper to taste
- 1 green onion, chopped for garnish

Instructions

1 Preheat your air fryer to 400°F.

2 In a small mixing bowl, combine the orange juice, soy sauce, rice vinegar, cornstarch, olive oil, ginger, salt, and pepper.

3 Toss the tofu cubes in the marinade, making sure they are evenly coated.

4 Place the tofu cubes in the air fryer basket and air fry for 12-15 minutes, or until crispy and golden brown.

5 Remove the tofu from the air fryer, and set aside.

6 In the same air fryer, add the slivered almonds and cook for 3-5 minutes or until golden brown.

7 In a large pan or wok, heat up 1 tablespoon of oil over high heat. Add the tofu to the pan and stir-fry for 2-3 minutes, or until heated through.

8 Add the orange zest and stir-fry for another minute.

9 Serve the stir fry over rice and garnish with the slivered almonds and green onions.

Nutritional Information (per serving):

- Calories: 365
- Total Fat: 25g
- Saturated Fat: 3g
- Cholesterol: 0mg
- Sodium: 597mg
- Total Carbohydrates: 18g
- Dietary Fiber: 4g   - Sugars: 8g   - Protein: 17g

24. Air Fryer Cajun-spiced Catfish

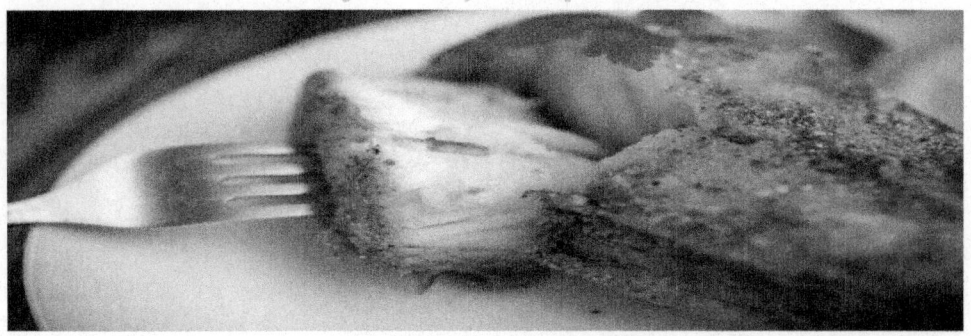

Ingredients

- 4 catfish fillets
- 1 teaspoon paprika
- 1 teaspoon cayenne pepper
- 1 teaspoon garlic powder
- 1 teaspoon onion powder
- 1 teaspoon dried oregano
- 1 teaspoon dried thyme
- 1/2 teaspoon salt
- 1/4 teaspoon black pepper
- 1 tablespoon olive oil
- Lemon wedges for serving

Instructions

1 Preheat your air fryer to 400°F.

2 Combine the paprika, cayenne pepper, garlic powder, onion powder, oregano, thyme, salt, and pepper in a small mixing bowl.

3 Rub the catfish fillets with olive oil and then coat them with the Cajun spice mixture.

4 Place the catfish fillets in the air fryer basket and air fry for 8-10 minutes or until the catfish is cooked through and flaky.

5 Serve the catfish with lemon wedges and enjoy!

Nutritional Information (per serving):

- Calories: 181
- Total Fat: 8g
- Saturated Fat: 2g
- Cholesterol: 68mg
- Sodium: 639mg
- Total Carbohydrates: 2g
- Dietary Fiber: 1g
- Sugars: 0g
- Protein: 25g

25. Lightened-up Broccoli and Cheese Soup

Ingredients

- 1 head of broccoli, chopped
- 1 onion, chopped
- 2 cloves of garlic, minced
- 2 cups of low-sodium chicken broth
- 1 cup of skim milk
- 1 cup of shredded cheddar cheese
- 1 tsp of olive oil
- Salt and pepper to taste

Instructions

1 Set the air fryer to 390 degrees Fahrenheit (200 degrees C).

2 n a pot of considerable size, warm up some olive oil on medium heat.

3 Add onion and garlic and sauté until softened.

4 Add chicken broth, skim milk, and broccoli to the pot. Bring the heat up to boiling, then reduce it to low. Simmer for 15-20 minutes or until broccoli is tender.

5 Cool the soup and then use an immersion blender to blend it until it is smooth.

6 Stir in shredded cheese until melted. Season with salt and pepper to taste.

7 Place the soup in the air fryer basket and cook for 10-15 minutes or until the top is golden and crispy.

Nutritional Information (per serving, based on 4 servings)

- Calories: 152
- Fat: 8g
- Saturated Fat: 4g
- Cholesterol: 23mg
- Sodium: 489mg
- Carbohydrates: 12g
- Fiber: 3g
- Sugar: 6g
- Protein: 10g

26. Turkey and Vegetable Meatloaf

Ingredients

- 1 lb ground turkey
- 1 cup grated zucchini
- 1/2 cup grated carrot
- 1/2 cup grated onion
- 1/2 cup rolled oats
- 1 egg
- 1 tsp dried thyme
- 1 tsp dried parsley
- Salt and pepper to taste
- 1/4 cup ketchup

Instructions

1 Set the air fryer to 390 degrees Fahrenheit (200 degrees C).

2 In a large bowl, mix together the ground turkey, grated zucchini, grated carrot, grated onion, rolled oats, egg, thyme, parsley, salt, and pepper.

3 Shape the mixture into a loaf and place it in the air fryer basket.

4 Spread ketchup on top of the loaf.

5 Cook in the air fryer for 30-40 minutes or until the internal temperature reaches 165 degrees F (74 degrees C).

Nutritional Information (per serving, based on 6 servings)

- Calories: 168
- Fat: 8g
- Saturated Fat: 2g
- Cholesterol: 92mg
- Sodium: 217mg
- Carbohydrates: 6g
- Fiber: 1g
- Sugar: 3g
- Protein: 18g

27. Air Fryer Turkey and Vegetable Chili

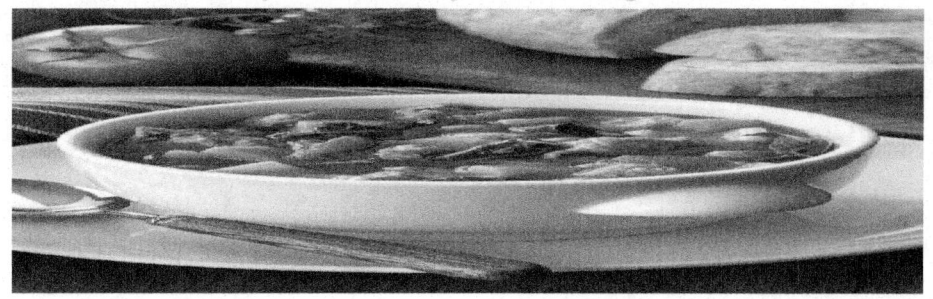

Ingredients

- 1 lb ground turkey
- 1 onion, diced
- 1 red bell pepper, diced
- 1 zucchini, diced
- 2 cloves of garlic, minced
- 1 can (14.5 oz) diced tomatoes
- 1 can (15 oz) kidney beans, drained and rinsed
- 1 cup of corn
- 2 tbsp chili powder
- 1 tsp cumin powder
- Salt and pepper to taste

Instructions

1 Set the air fryer to 390 degrees Fahrenheit (200 degrees C).

2 In a large pot, brown the ground turkey over medium heat until cooked through. Drain any excess fat.

3 Add the onion, red bell pepper, zucchini, and garlic to the pot and sauté for 3-5 minutes or until softened.

4 Stir in the diced tomatoes, kidney beans, corn, chili powder, cumin powder, salt, and pepper. Bring the mixture to a simmer and cook for 10-15 minutes or until the vegetables are tender.

5 Place the chili mixture in the air fryer basket and cook for 10-15 minutes or until the top is golden and crispy.

Nutritional Information (per serving, based on 4 servings)

- Calories: 264
- Fat: 8g
- Saturated Fat: 2g
- Cholesterol: 72mg
- Sodium: 556mg
- Carbohydrates: 28g
- Fiber: 7g
- Sugar: 7g
- Protein: 22g

28. Grilled Lemon-Garlic Chicken and Vegetables

Ingredients

- 2 cups of mixed vegetables (such as bell peppers, zucchini, and mushrooms)
- 2 cloves of garlic, minced
- 2 lemons, juiced
- 2 tablespoons of olive oil
- 4 boneless, skinless chicken breasts
- Salt and pepper to taste

Instructions

Directions:

1 Lemon juice, minced garlic, olive oil, salt, and pepper should all be combined in a small bowl.

2 Place the chicken breasts in a large reseal-able plastic bag and pour the marinade over the chicken. Coat the chicken evenly by sealing the bag and tossing it. Place the item in the refrigerator and allow it to marinate for a minimum of 30 minutes.

3 400°F should be the air fryer's set temperature.

4 Place the marinated chicken and vegetables in the air fryer basket and cook for 15-20 minutes, or until the chicken is cooked through.

5 Serve and enjoy.

Nutritional Information (per serving):

- Calories: 270
- Protein: 34g
- Carbohydrates: 7g
- Fat: 12g
- Sodium: 80mg
- Fiber: 2g
- Sugars: 3g

29. Air Fryer Sausage and Pepper Hoagies

Ingredients

- 4 hoagie rolls
- 4-6 fully cooked low-fat chicken sausage links
- 1/2 teaspoon Italian seasoning
- 1/2 green bell pepper, thinly sliced
- 1/4 cup finely diced onion
- 1/2 teaspoon garlic powder
- 1/4 teaspoon crushed red pepper flakes
- 1/2 red bell pepper, thinly sliced
- 2 tablespoons olive oil
- Salt and pepper, to taste
- 4 slices reduced-fat mozzarella cheese

Instructions

1 Set the temperature of your air fryer to 400 F.

2 Slice the hoagie rolls in half, lengthwise, and set aside.

3 In a bowl, mix together bell peppers, onion, garlic powder, Italian seasoning, crushed red pepper flakes, olive oil, salt and pepper until evenly combined..

4 Place the sausage links in the air fryer and cook for 8 minutes.

5 Remove the sausage links from the air fryer and slice them into 1/2-inch pieces.

6 Place the sliced sausage and the bell pepper mixture in the air fryer and cook for 8 minutes.

7 Place the hoagie rolls in the air fryer and cook for 2 minutes.

8 Remove the rolls from the air fryer and place the sausage and pepper mixture on top of the rolls.

- Top with the mozzarella cheese and cook for an additional 2 minutes.
- Serve warm. Enjoy.

Nutritional Information:

- Serving Size: 1 hoagie
- Calories: 450
- Fat: 22g
- Carbohydrates: 31g
- Protein: 28g
- Sodium: 795mg
- Sugar: 5g

30. Chicken and Vegetable Paella

Ingredients

- 1 tablespoon olive oil
- 2 cloves garlic, minced
- 1 onion, diced
- 1 red bell pepper, diced
- 1 cup uncooked long grain white rice
- 2 cups low-sodium chicken broth
- 1/2 teaspoon saffron threads
- 1/2 teaspoon smoked paprika
- 1/2 teaspoon dried oregano
- 1/2 teaspoon kosher salt
- 1/4 teaspoon freshly ground black pepper
- 2 boneless, skinless chicken breasts, cut into bite-sized pieces
- 1 cup frozen peas
- 1 (14.5-ounce) can of diced tomatoes
- 1/4 cup sliced green olives

Instructions

1 Heat the air fryer to 375°F.

2 In a nonstick skillet, heat the olive oil over medium heat Add the garlic, onion, and bell pepper, and cook until softened, about 5 minutes.

3 dd the rice, chicken broth, saffron, paprika, oregano, salt, and pepper. Stir to combine.

4 Transfer the mixture to the air fryer and cook for 15 minutes.

5 Add the chicken, peas, and tomatoes. Stir to combine. Cook for an additional 10 minutes.

6 Stir in the olives, and cook for an additional 5 minutes.

7 Serve hot.

Nutritional Information:

- Servings: 6
- Calories: 293
- Fat: 7g
- Carbohydrates: 28g
- Protein: 23g
- Fiber: 3g- Sugar: 4g- Sodium: 509mg

CONCLUSION
The Benefits of Using an Air Fryer for Diabetic Cooking

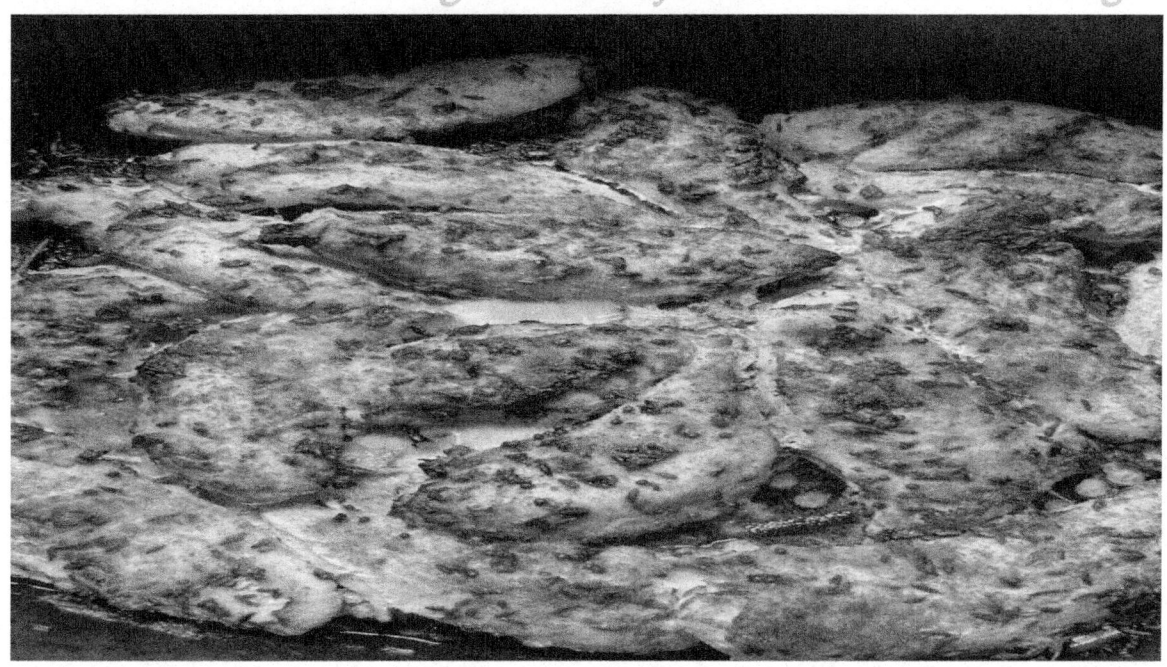

Cooking with an air fryer can be a game-changer for individuals with diabetes who are looking to improve their dietary habits and manage their blood sugar levels. Air fryers are versatile kitchen appliances that use hot air and a small amount of oil to cook food, resulting in meals that are lower in fat and calories compared to traditional deep-frying methods. This makes them an ideal tool for individuals with diabetes who are looking to prepare healthy and delicious meals.

One of the main benefits of using an air fryer for diabetic cooking is that it can help to reduce the overall fat content of meals. Traditional deep-frying methods require a large amount of oil, which can add a significant amount of fat and calories to food. Air fryers, on the other hand, use a small amount of oil, typically just a few tablespoons, which can reduce the fat content of meals by up to 80%. This can help to prevent weight gain and improve overall health, which is important for individuals with diabetes.

Air fryers also help to retain the natural flavors and nutrients of food, making them an ideal tool for preparing healthy and delicious meals. Traditional deep-frying methods can cause food to lose its natural flavors and nutrients, resulting in meals that are less nutritious. Air fryers, on the other hand, cook food using hot air, which helps to preserve the natural flavors and nutrients of the food. This makes it an ideal tool for preparing healthy and delicious meals for individuals with diabetes.

Another benefit of using an air fryer for diabetic cooking is that it can help to reduce the overall carbohydrate content of meals. Many traditional deep-frying methods, such as breading and battering, can add a significant amount of carbohydrates to food. Air fryers, on the other hand, can be used to prepare meals that are low in carbohydrates, making them an ideal tool for individuals with diabetes who are looking to manage their blood sugar levels

The appliance itself is also easy to use and maintain. The appliance is simple to operate and the non-stick coating of the basket makes the cleaning process much easier. Also, air fryers come in different sizes and features, so it's easy to find one that fits your kitchen and your needs.

Using an air fryer for diabetic cooking can provide numerous benefits, including reducing the overall fat and carbohydrate content of meals, retaining the natural flavors and nutrients of food, and making it easy to use and maintain. By incorporating an air fryer into their cooking routine, individuals with diabetes can improve their dietary habits and better manage their blood sugar levels, leading to an overall improvement in their health and well-being.

Key Takeaways from the Book
Overview of the Different Recipes and Meal Ideas Featured in the Book

The "Diabetic Air Fryer Cookbook for Beginners" features a wide variety of delicious, healthy, and low-carb recipes and meal ideas that are specifically tailored to the dietary needs of individuals with diabetes. The book is designed to provide readers with a wealth of inspiration and ideas for using an air fryer to prepare meals that are not only delicious, but also nutritious and beneficial for managing blood sugar levels.

The book starts off with a section on breakfast recipes, including options such as Air Fryer Cinnamon French Toast Sticks, Air Fryer Breakfast Burritos, and Air Fryer Blueberry Muffins. These recipes are a great way to start the day with a healthy and satisfying meal that is low in carbohydrates and packed with nutrients.

The book then moves on to a section on main dishes, featuring recipes such as Air Fryer Baked Chicken, Air Fryer Shrimp Scampi, and Air Fryer Meatloaf. These recipes are perfect for dinner and are easy to prepare and delicious. The author also includes different options for vegetarians and vegans.

The book also features a section on side dishes, including options such as Air Fryer Roasted Vegetables, Air Fryer Sweet Potato Fries, and Air Fryer Parmesan Garlic Brussels Sprouts. These recipes are a great way to add a healthy and delicious side dish to any meal and are packed with nutrients.

The book concludes with a section on desserts, featuring recipes such as Air Fryer Apple Chips, Air Fryer Chocolate Chip Cookies, and Air Fryer Blueberry Crisp. These recipes are a great way to satisfy a sweet tooth without compromising on nutrition. The author also includes some options for those who are following a ketogenic diet.The "Diabetic Air Fryer Cookbook for Beginners" offers a wide variety of recipes and meal ideas that are perfect for individuals with diabetes. The book provides readers with a wealth of inspiration and ideas for using an air fryer to prepare delicious, healthy, and low-carb meals that are tailored to their specific dietary needs. Whether you're looking for breakfast, lunch, or dinner options, or even dessert, this book has something for everyone.

Tips and Tricks for Using an Air Fryer Effectively in Diabetic Cooking

An air fryer can be a great tool for individuals with diabetes who are looking to improve their cooking skills and prepare healthy and delicious meals. However, like any kitchen appliance, it can take some time to learn how to use it effectively. The "Diabetic Air Fryer Cookbook for Beginners" provides readers with a wealth of tips and tricks for using an air fryer effectively in diabetic cooking, making it an essential guide for anyone who is new to using this appliance.

One of the first tips for using an air fryer effectively in diabetic cooking is to choose the right air fryer for your needs. Not all air fryers are created equal, and it's important to choose one that is the right size for your kitchen and your cooking needs. The book provides readers with guidance on how to select the right air fryer, including information on the different types of air fryers available and their unique features.

Another important tip for using an air fryer effectively in diabetic cooking is to properly maintain and clean the appliance. Air fryers can be a bit tricky to clean, but the book provides readers with detailed instructions on how to properly clean and maintain the appliance, including tips on how to remove stubborn stains and prevent build-up.

When it comes to preparing food, it's essential to use the right amount of oil and to choose the right type of oil. Air fryers are designed to cook food with a minimal amount of oil, but it's important to use the right amount of oil to ensure that food is cooked evenly and doesn't stick to the basket. The book provides guidance on how to use the right amount of oil and which types of oil are best for different types of food.

Another important tip for using an air fryer effectively in diabetic cooking is to learn how to properly adjust the temperature and cooking time. Air fryers cook food using hot air, and it's important to learn how to properly adjust the temperature and cooking time to ensure that food is cooked evenly and to perfection. The book provides guidance on how to properly adjust the temperature and cooking time, and it also includes cooking charts that can be used as a reference.

It's important to be aware of the different foods that are suitable for air fryer cooking. Some foods may not be suitable for air fryer cooking, and it's important to learn how to choose the right foods and prepare them properly. The book provides guidance on how to choose the right foods for air fryer cooking, and it also includes tips on how to prepare different types of food for air fryer cooking.

Personal Reflection

Printed in Great Britain
by Amazon